Death, My Guidance (

PART 1 - My Story

Imagine you're playing a football game. The Champions League final; 90 minutes.
Everything is riding on it.
The clock crosses the 90th minute and it's still 0-0.
Injury Time.
You don't know how long this is going to last. The ref could blow his whistle at
any moment, and you have no control over when that happens. Once he does, there
is absolutely nothing else you can do to help get the result you so badly want.

Welcome to my world.

Ever since January 6th 2011, I have felt like I've been living on borrowed time –
on injury time – not knowing when the ref was going to blow his whistle, and
when my time on this planet would be up.

Why, you ask?

Well, to understand that, we've got to go back a few years…

Ever since I was about 4 years old, the only thing I ever thought about doing was
being a professional rugby player. I was good. Not a superstar, but I always
believed that in the right position, with the right amount of work, it could have
been possible. After all, of the 22 people I last played with in school, something
like 13 of them went on to get paid for playing rugby within 3 years. Mad.

That was in my final year in school. Instead of staying in Ireland, though, I went
down to Australia to see the world, and to change my position in rugby from wing
to flanker.

Oh, and to train.
A lot.

I worked and lived in St Josephs College in Sydney, Australia. Gardening, doing
the mail, supervising study and the boarders…it was a pretty cruisy job, taking up
about 20 hours a week and paying me enough to go out 4 nights a week and buy
all the protein and creatine powders I'd need.

My daily routine looked something like this:

7am – Up. Hill sprints. A lot of them.

8am – Breakfast – 12 Weetabix and ~5 eggs, every day.
9am – Work in school, 2 hours.
11am – Upper-body workout, followed by protein and creatine.
12.30 – Lunch. ~1,500 calories.
2pm – Lower-body workout, protein & creatine.
4 – Work, 2 hours
6 – Dinner - ~1,500 cals.
8 – Work, 2 hours.

9pm – Buy a bottle of Southern Comfort and drink it all before going out – 4 nights/7
OR, Go to bed, wake up at 2am to do 30 minutes core workout followed by protein, before going back to bed before hill-sprints at 7am the next day.

Round and round I'd go, keeping up this routine for 6 months. The teachers in the school asked me 3 times to stop and really reconsider the long term consequences of what I was doing, but I really was in a trance-like state, not taking any wisdom in unless it was going to help with my training.

Unsurprisingly, maybe, it all did end up catching up with me.

6 months in, I had put on almost 15 kilograms of lean muscle mass from this regime. I had fought through bouts of sleep deprivation and felt that with my new, extreme athleticism, I was ready for a great season of rugby in Australia before heading back to Ireland to follow my dream.

Unfortunately, nature had other plans…

NZ Timeline

January 1st 2011

Myself, Harry, Dermot and Will – my 3 school friends with whom I had moved to Australia and worked – all arrived in Auckland to begin our 3-week 'Kiwi Experience' tour of New Zealand over the Christmas break. The trip of a life time. With Skydiving, Bungee Jumping, Canyon Swings and Jet Boating all lined up, this was bound to be the best holiday of our lives.

January 5th 2011

After 3 days in Paihia in the Bay of Islands north of Auckland, chilling, jet-skiing and witnessing the wildlife – which included a terrified-of-sharks Harry Fehily splashing around in fear after falling off his jet-ski – we arrive back in Auckland before heading to Rotorua the next day. We don't go out, just hang in the hostel and go to bed early. I wake up during the night to a terrible stink in our hostel room.
Surprisingly, I'm not the cause this time.

Myself and Dermot, who is also awake with the smell, identify the source as the feet of a Swedish guy in our room. Outrageous.

We go up and try to wake him but he's out in a drunken slumber, so we get his towel and wrap it around his feet to keep the smell in. He wakes up the next morning, tries to walk away from his bed and falls over, and the discussion ensues. No hard feelings, we all laugh it off and he's embarrassed about his feet!

We go get breakfast around 9am and are ready at our bus at 10. We get onboard and drive out of Auckland. We stop for photographs at a hill overlooking Eden Park stadium and, from there, embark on our 2 hour journey to Rotorua, where skydiving and several other adventure sports await us.

Still exhausted after a terrible nights' sleep the night before, I decide to go for a nap on the bus so that I could arrive in Rotorua with a bit of energy.

I didn't know at the time that that was very nearly the last decision I ever made…

11.00 am

A short while into my sleep, the lads I was with started to notice that I was breathing very strangely. At first, they thought I was doing it deliberately to draw attention to them from the other passengers on the bus. Then, after throwing an iPhone at my head and getting zero reaction from me, they started to take more notice. I had gone completely blue, and my upper body had started to buckle over, as no oxygen was getting in.

I was in the middle of a cardiac arrest. I was dying right in front of them

They freaked out. Truth be told, they froze for a minute. They were 18 year old kids on a holiday with their friend, who, at almost 120kg and 10% body fat, was at that point a picture of good health and strength; who two hours earlier was laughing with the Swedes over breakfast…was this really happening?

Luckily, they snapped out of it and shouted for the bus to be stopped. It was the drivers first day on the job, no joke.
Poor guy.
They carried me off. They still give me shit about how much effort that took. They lay me out on the ground and a German nurse, who just happened to be onboard the bus, showed them how to give me CPR while they waited for the ambulance to show up.
It took 12 minutes – the amount of time for which I was clinically dead.
The guys gave me CPR interchangeably – you'd be surprised how tiring it is (apparently). We were such meatheads at the time that one of them was even on steroids. This is relevant because when he was giving me CPR compressions, he actually cracked my rib. I still, every morning, have to crack it back into place today.

The ambulance came. The crowd made way, and within seconds they were cutting open my jumper to expose my bare chest. They immediately began administering shocks to me with an external defibrillator.

"Clear!", charge, SHOCK!
"Clear!", charge, SHOCK!
"Clear!", charge, SHOCK!
"Clear!", charge, SHOCK!
"Clear!", charge, SHOCK!

Five shocks, still no breath. One more…

"Clear!", charge, SHOCK!

Nothing.

Looking up at the lads, the medic says that I'm gone. They put me in the ambulance.

Now, usually, too many shocks from a defibrillator can fry your brain and leave the patient with brain damage, if the body can't absorb all of the electricity. What dawned on these medics, though, was that I had added roughly 25kg of padding to my natural frame that would enable me to absorb more. It was risky behaviour and left me with a very high chance of being left with brain damage, but they deemed it worthwhile to administer me with some incremental shocks in the back of the ambulance.

"Clear!", charge, SHOCK!
"Clear!", charge, SHOCK!
"Clear!", charge, SHOCK!
"Clear!", charge, SHOCK!
"Clear!", charge, SHOCK!

Five more shocks. They felt a pulse. I was back alive. Now they just needed to get me into an induced coma as fast as they could before the lack of oxygen to my brain meant that I was really fucked.

They burst through the doors of Middlemore Hospital with me laid out on the stretcher and brought me into the theatre of Dr David Heaven.
Now I can't imagine any doctor screwing around when they've got a dead 18 year old laid out in front of them, but I feel lucky that David Heaven was in that day because above all things, he was known for being ice-cold under pressure. He got me into a coma just in the nick of time did everything else that was necessary to fit me into the tiny odds I had of surviving.

Here's the worst part. When the lads reached the hospital and saw that I was in the hands of the doctors, they looked at each other blankly as they all reached the same realisation:

Someone was going to have to call my family to tell them I had dropped dead.

Harry and Will called their parents to get their advice on speaking to mine, while Dermot called my only brother, Rob, who is 3 years older than me. I have never been able to imagine what it would have been like on either end of that phone call, and frankly, I prefer to not try to.

When my parents heard the news, they booked the next flight down to Auckland. Via Hong Kong. They left 24 hours later and were in HK roughly 8 hours after that. When they got to HK for the stopover, they called the hospital to get an update on my condition.

They'd still just be coming down to pick up my body, they were told.

This was two days into the coma.

On day 3, about a day after my parents arrived, I took a turn for the better, and it actually looked like I'd recover. The next day, more improvement. The day after that, more. On the sixth day of the coma, then, I woke up. I total freaked out and, remembering that I was a lot bigger back then, I just got up and tried to leave the hospital. Doctors tried to stop me and I just started swinging. I actually landed on one of them and they got sent home. I don't remember any of this. I can't even imagine how confused I must have been.

Eventually, the hospital security was called and two giant Samoans appeared. That was the end of that, and I was back in my bed within minutes! To prevent such an episode from happening again, though, this time I was tied to the bed with a rope. No getting up this time!

Throughout all of this, I couldn't speak. Between the large number of shocks and the hypothermic state of being in a coma for a working week, my brain had effectively been fried and frozen. I slurred my speech as I tried to construct mumbling sentences that made even less sense than usual. My guess is that I resembled some sort of a drowsy, baby-faced, gym-going Frankenstein with tubes coming out of every side of him.

Dermot came in to tell me that I'd never be able to play rugby or train intensely again.

Poor me, you might think. Poor him, though, really. My brain was so fried that I had no short term memory and I still didn't understand what had happened –
Dermo had to have that conversation with me about 12 times over the next 3 days, each and every one of which caused me to freak out and break down. Rugby. Sport. Training intensely. These were the only things I knew and loved. These were the only things that fed into any of my goals for life.

This is all very gloomy. There were, believe it or not, some very funny moments had in the hospital. The first thing I did when I woke up from the coma was ask my mom if we could go for a steak in my favourite restaurant in Drogheda, not knowing that my favourite restaurant was about 18,000km away.

After that, they had to test for brain damage on the long-term memory with some simple questions. Mom, being the mother that she is, insisted that she be the one to ask the questions. First up:

"Ok honey, what's your name?"
I look at her.
"Francois".
She turns to the doctor, who nods toward me as if to say 'go again'.

'Ok. And what is your address, sweetheart?"
"Number 66, Rue Saint Catrine, Bordeaux", I say.
She wells up. Her little boy has brain damage.

When I see the panic on her face, I fess up.
"Mom, Mom, I'm kidding!" I say. I say my name and my address and I ask if we can go and get that steak.

Easily the most inappropriate joke I have ever cracked, and that's saying something!

We go through the week, trying to get my speech back and get me walking around again. I remember one day where we get some pizzas in to the hospital and I eat them with the 3 guys. At that point I still had a while to go but they were encouraged by my ability to still slag Harry having just come out of a coma. Priorities.

A week went by, I had a pacemaker/defibrillator put in and was discharged from hospital. Another week went by and I was flown by the insurance company to Ireland to recover and get on with my life. The problem was, I didn't know what that was going to look like now that sport was gone.

Oh, and I also didn't have a short term memory, but that was just my little secret.

I spent the next two months trying to recover physically and emotionally from the whole thing. People were pretty happy to see that I was still alive and that I was going to be ok, and I kept up the appearance during the day. Truthfully, though, I spent the next two months crying myself to sleep every night – partly because I could never do the only thing I'd ever wanted to do, partly because I couldn't even train at a serious rate again (or so I was being told), and partly because I had a pretty damaged short term memory that I was afraid to tell anyone about because I had already brought them through so much.

There was nothing I could do about the first two problems. The third, I had to change. I took an athlete's approach. If I wanted bigger arms, I'd do curls. Bigger legs, I'd do deadlifts. If I wanted a short term memory, surely I could do whatever the resistance exercise for that was – learning a language. I'd always been in love with Spain and fancied their women, so I decided to increase my chances with them by learning Spanish online using a course called Fluenz, which is similar to Rosetta Stone. Of the 7 hours a day I now had free from not being able to train, I put roughly half of them into learning Spanish for the first two months. The short-term memory had healed and a new passion was born – learning Spanish.

For the next three years of college I was extremely confused – I tried countless different sports:

Boxing – made the university team but got kicked out when they saw the pacemaker.
Kickboxing – got kneed about 2 inches away from the pacemaker, had it hit the device I could have died.
Triathlon – was told I couldn't do this because of the high heart rate.
Marathon – same thing – got to 25k runs and stopped.
Rowing – heart rate.
Fencing – saw it in a movie and booked a class the next morning.
Tennis – childhood sport.
Golf – childhood sport.
Windsurfing – cousins got me into it. Love it but I'm crap.
Wakeboarding – current favourite, loving it. Still crap!
Sea Swimming – had a mini-panic attack in the water last month. Bit dangerous for me but I love it.
Surfing – did it a fair bit in Australia. Got wiped out one time and the fin on the surf board nearly usurped the pacemaker. Not good.
Salsa Dancing – Loved doing this is Sydney. At 6'5, I'm not quite slick enough for it but it's great craic!
Hip Hop dancing – I did a course in Sydney and am thinking about doing one again in Dublin. It was just me and a load of pregnant women in this class which was strange but was a pretty funny picture!

Today, I just go to the gym, do some yoga (getting really into that), and play golf and get outdoors swimming, hiking and rockclimbing - more on the outdoors later.

Last year I went through about 7 months of Post Traumatic Stress Disorder after nearly passing away on my own in a gym after my heart rate reached 261bpm on a morning run. 7 months of panic attacks and night terrors on an almost daily basis was enough to take me to a pretty low place. This inspired me to start an events business, quit my job at Google, and then go and travel South America for 3 months on my own. I walked a path which I had no idea where it would take me…and I still don't… but I know that walking fearlessly into that unknown is what enabled me to conquer the PTSD and move forward. It is what enabled me to come home and start this business and doing the things I'm doing now, and it is what enabled me to go from the lowest point of my life around June 2017 to the highest in June 2018.

Why did the cardiac arrest happen in the first place? Nobody knows. All we can say is that I have Sudden Adult Death Syndrome, which is about as fun a thing to say about yourself as you can imagine it is.

But I can say this with my hand, pardon the pun, on my heart: the cardiac arrest has been easily the best thing that's happened in my life. It has cleaned up my family – inspiring a separation of my parents that really should have happened years ago. It opened my eyes to a world outside of sport, and a world that is much more multidimensional than the worlds that anyone else I know sees. It has turned me from a very ambitious person into an extremely ambitious person, making me fearless against anything that life can throw at me as I aim to do the things and have the impact that I know I can have. It has inspired me to love, laugh and live as intensely as I can, knowing that that referees whistle could suddenly blow at any moment…

My Relationship with Death

I know this is a weird thing to talk openly about, so let me just set the context and let you know when my relationship with Death began.

Before the cardiac arrest, when I was just an abnormally sporty 18 year old, I had less of a relationship with Death than even the average person. I was so convinced that I was physically invincible that the idea that something could happen to me – let alone a sudden cardiac arrest while asleep on a bus on my holidays – just never even crossed my mind.

Then, on the 6th of January at 11am on the road to Rotorua, Death appeared. The thing is, I didn't see him. He got me while I was asleep, and by the time my friends had noticed, I was already gone. It was in the hospital, when I woke and was told that I had had an interaction with him, that I started to get rattled. I digested this over the next couple of months and, truthfully, years.

Why had he come for me?
Did I not deserve the rest of my life?
Was I living so wrong that it was better to take me off the planet?
What was meant for my family and friends that they had to go through the pain of losing a loved one in order to reach or achieve it?

And most importantly…the question I still ask myself:

What does the gift of my survival mean? Death granted me a favour, what favour is expected of me in return? It's a genuine question, because if there's one thing I've learned, it's that Death doesn't play games. Death doesn't play small hands. When Death is at the table, everyone is all in and showing all their cards, whether they want to or not. Death forces a person to examine every single aspect of his or her life – openly with others – to try to evaluate it before they move on to the next place.

So that's what I did. I had to go all in. If I'm honest, I might well have been so short sighted and blind to the bigger picture that, had I not had the pacemaker put in, I would have gone back to focussing on rugby. I don't know. But thankfully, my path was such that I would be absolutely prohibited from doing that or any other intense sport ever again. That's where the pain was. What the fuck was I going to do with my life? Why bother letting me survive if the only theme of my life was the only theme I couldn't play to?

This is where the idea of Death as a Guidance Counsellor came in.

Throughout the past 8 years, as my heart has flared up at different times, Death has stepped in and taught me a lesson or encouraged me to change direction. Quit drinking. Always get a good night's sleep. Don't waste precious time on earth. Invest intensely in relationships because they're the source of magic down here. Identify where you get your belly laughs and keep going back there. These are all lessons that have been taught along the way. Then, last year, when I was running on January 26 and my heart rate reached 261bpm, I was really sure I was going to die alone in that gym. It was just me and Death in there. That's when he spoke loudest and clearest and specifically about my career and how I was spending my time.

"Write a book – it's something you've been pondering for a while now. Start that events business you've been day-dreaming about. Get out of Google, you don't want to be there. Go to South America, it's always been a dream of yours. Go back to Ireland. It's time."

Bang, bang, bang, bang, bang.

5 clear messages addressing the dreams and bucket list items that I'd been dreaming and wondering about for months and even years by that point. That was the most powerful wake-up call to live the life I actually wanted to live that I'd ever received. What's more, he followed up. Creeping into my mind every day, threatening to take me then and there. Breathing down my neck as I tried to go to sleep. And once I did, the night terrors were so bad that my house mate Harry – yep, same Harry – was running into my room with a golf club, four nights a week, thinking I was getting attacked! Last April an Uber driver had to help me get up off the side walk I was lying on and put me in his car – I was crippled by fear and couldn't walk another step. Harry was helping me up stair cases. It was crazy.

But it was motivating. I did all the things I wanted to do. I ran at everything the PTSD had made me afraid of and I ventured out into the abyss when I went to South America – not knowing if I'd ever leave that continent, or if I'd ever get my career back on track.
But I'd been dead. I'd suffered secretly through brain damage for 2 months. I'd suffered semi-secretly through PTSD for 7 months and I'd watched my family break up from close range. What else could the world do to me that was going to be any worse than those things?? Strange as it may sound, Death taught me not to be afraid. It taught me that there's nothing to be afraid *of*!

Why did Death choose me?

Honestly? I think it's because he couldn't find a teenager who was more certain about what he wanted out of life, or who was doing more to achieve it than I was. Knocking that teenager off his path and dropping him into a psychological and emotional blender for five years might prove to be an interesting experiment (or, you know, a sick joke). I was a good communicator. Maybe he figured that if I could come out of that blender with my head in-tact that I'd have a message to share? Maybe, I don't know. But that's the angle I'm going with.

And this book? I guess this is my attempt at sharing that message. Now there might be one or two things in here that you will think of as clichés. I hope not, but not everything in this book is an original thought that I have had. Yes, I reached all of these conclusions absolutely independently, but I acknowledge that – with several of them – I wasn't exactly the first person to reach that conclusion. Unfortunately, in some of these cases, it did take me dropping dead and processing that for eight years to finally have the lesson sink in, and I'm just trying to help you avoid that fate, so here goes…

Part 2 – The Self

So that's me. Now let's talk about you. The reason 'The Self' comes before 'Careers' and 'Beyond the Self' in this book is because that is the order in which we need to get our shit together. Get your Self right. Get a good understanding of who *you* are, who you have been, who you want to be, who you are actually becoming, and what the difference between all those people is. Life may happen around us, but if it is all perceived and experienced inside our head, and if who we are to our immediate surroundings is what triggers the nature of everything in our life, then really, the most important things for us to manage are these:

1) How we perceive the world that we interact with, day to day
2) Who we are to that world, and what we give to *it* to perceive

That's what all of this is about. I'm confident that you should finish this book with a deeper understanding of yourself than you had when you picked it up (or downloaded it), having been challenged on a lot of the points that we as young people should be challenged on, and optimistic about your own abilities to overcome these and any other challenges that you'll face going forward, not least because you'll have a better understanding of why you want and need to overcome them.

Good luck!

Fast Day is a Good Day

My house mate came in from work the other day. I asked him how the day was. He said it was great. I asked why. His answer struck me:
"Because it went nice and quick', he said.
Oh Dear.
On your last day on Earth, there will be one thing you want. Just one thing: One more day. When you're old and grey, you will say, countless times, that would do anything for just one day as a free, young, healthy 22, 24, 26, 28 year old.

Why is it then, that right in the middle of these glory days, we are literally wishing the days away? It's crazy! We should be doing the opposite! We should be looking for our youth, our freedom and our boundless energy to last as long as we can, because one day, not so long from now, we'll be woken up by the sound of a crying baby or a call from a boss saying you're needed back in work at 9 o'clock at night, and you'll pause for a minute. wondering where the years and the freedom went.

Honestly, my housemates' answer made me sad for him. He's since quit that job, thank God, and has gone travelling the world and making use of his health and freedom, and that makes both of us so happy. But when he gets back to work, I hope he looks for a job that he will actually enjoy on some level. That will stimulate him and tickle his brain just enough that he won't be counting down the clock on the remainder of his youth, in the knowledge that he will wake up less than ten years from now and realise that he no longer has that same freedom.

And I wish the same for you. If, for you, a fast day is a good day, you are living someone else's life and you need to change.

2 Acts – Committed Life

I have learned that, while life is nothing more than a compilation of phases that we go through, there are two, broad 'macro phases' that underlie all others. These two macro phases, or Acts, occur in the same order, every time. They are:

Act I: Search
Act II: Create

Act 1- The Search

The Search Act usually consists of the first quarter or third of our life. We explore the world, we explore our relationships, and we explore ourselves.

Why?

Because we are searching. We are searching for everything. As kids, we are searching for understanding of what is going on around us, we are searching for interaction and love from friends and family, we are searching for threats to our survival and we are searching for things that stimulate us, that we consider to be fun.
Moving into our teenage years, then, we start to search on a slightly deeper level. We search for understanding of the opposite sex, we search for understanding of our own hormones, feelings and drivers. We search for hobbies to provide us with consistent challenge, stimulation and opportunity for growth and / or glory.
Next, as we enter adulthood, we start to search for meaning in our lives. We search for ideals to look up to, for causes to apply our time and talent to, and for challenges that can show us where our strengths and weaknesses are. One thing I can tell you from experience here, is that idealism without action is just frustration. If you have ideals that you feel strongly about, let your actions reflect them. If they don't, you will only grow frustrated and bitter.

We also – many of us – search for spiritual guidance, or at least for our spiritual selves to be met by some community, practice or belief system. This search is particularly prevalent given the decline in popularity of structured religion in the modern world.
Next, then, we search for avenues in which to achieve some permanence and consistency. We look for partners, soul mates, lasting relationships and loves. We look for jobs and causes that we can commit to for a lasting period of time. Many of us start looking for a family of our own and a means of creating that.
In a nutshell, this is the point at which we start looking to create, and creation requires commitment.

One important thing about the Search Act is that it sounds much cooler and easier than it is. I can imagine you sitting there now, reading this and thinking 'wait, so my only responsibility right now is to explore and not worry about permanence?'

But it's not that is easy. In fact, the Search phase is extremely hard, when done right. Doing it right looks a little something like this:

- You search *hard*. You don't just casually wander around the planet getting baked and sleeping around. And if you do do that, you have to process it right. Processing is the key here. What are you learning about what you look for in relationships? How is that evolving? What jobs have you liked and not liked so far? Why and why not? What have you seen or experienced that has made you really excited /fascinated? What do these things have in common? What cause have you heard or read about that has really moved you and made you think? What do you have that you can offer to that cause? The questions are endless.
Searching hard will see you go down roads, get very excited about what might lie at the end of them, and then get told unexpectedly that it's a dead end and that you have to turn back. So far, this has happened to me with one relationship, one business, and about 5 sports, and every single time it has almost broken me. Not fun.

- You prioritise the search. In order to live out the Search Act as well as can be done, you must prioritise the search. Too many people end up in jobs, relationships and lives they don't like because their search became a low priority for them. They committed themselves to these things without actually knowing themselves very well. Sure, your Self will always be changing and evolving– there's a great saying that the same man never got into the same river twice, because the river had always changed and the man had always changed – but the core will always be there. Get to know what that core is made up of and then start to committing to things. Do it prematurely and you will be unhappy at your core – worst possible outcome.

  Security matters. Security matters in everything, but above all, perhaps, security matters in career. I don't deny that. I totally acknowledge and value it. What I don't value, though, is when someone stays in a job they don't like, and uses the reason that they're doing it for their kids or their family (whether they have one or not). I see that line of logic. Hell, I used to talk like that myself while I was in investment banking. What I have realised recently though, just from talking to friends and strangers, is this: When someone is talking about their parents and what it is they appreciate about them – they never talk about their job title or their money. I mean never, not once.
  What does this tell you?
  Well what it tells me, is that when we focus on what we can be for our family, we are focussing on the wrong thing. What we should be focussing on – the things that families *really* appreciate – is *who* we can be for them, and that brings about a whole different approach to life.

I could be a wealthy banker who can send his kids to the finest schools and take them on amazing holidays, absolutely. That's great! The downside? I might never be there. I might have a poor relationship with my wife because I'm never there. Else, I might often be there, just as much as any other dad, but I've spent the past twenty years of my life doing something that I'm not really passionate about or interested in, and my appreciation of the world may have eroded away. My zest for life may have gone and I may not give the energy or wonder or sense of magic to my kids that would really light up their childhood. See what I mean?

On the other hand, I might be a college lecturer (secret dream of mine) and make 20% of the money I'd make in a bank. But I love my job, I love my wife, and together with her, I have the energy and appreciation of the world around me to provide my kids with a loving, magical and encouraging family culture; one that fuels their own passions and interests and gives them a fantastic childhood. Now that, to me, is the ultimate achievement.

I'll be honest with you. I grew up around money. I went to one of the best schools in Ireland, I have seen the insides of the homes of a hundred families that have taken the first path described above – a very honourable thing to do I might highlight, focussing on providing for your family – and I can tell you that the family cultures often suffer from exactly what I've described.

This isn't a theory. I haven't made this up. It's evidenced-based. I've seen this in real life – at scale - and this is what happens. The kids I have known to come out of happy homes – regardless of material wealth above breadline – have grown into some of the most successful adults I know.

If I were to put all this in a nutshell, I guess I'd just summarise by saying that the best thing you can do for your kids is not provide them with 'all the opportunity in the world', it is to provide them with a happy, loving home that encourages them to love and explore the world themselves, and that can only be done if you have done the same and if you yourself are truly happy. Completing a thorough search is a key element of that.

- Perform the Search outside your comfort zone. Cliché, so I'll keep it short. There are many great things about your comfort zone, and there will be plenty of times in your life when the best thing for you to do will be to enjoy those things within your comfort zone. Now is not one of those times. The comfort zone is a zone built on answers. The Search is made up of questions. The Search is about growth. Your comfort zone provides you with 0% growth rate. Clear answers to the hardest questions are the foundation of a fruitful life. If you stay in your comfort zone, you will never even learn what the questions are, let alone what the answers are for you.

I have been very lucky in my life to have been blessed with a sudden death at 18, brain damage, the loss of all my dreams, post-traumatic stress disorder, a broken-up family and the loss of all my confidence combined with homesickness on the other side of the world. These things have all kept me well outside of any comfort zone and asking some of life's hardest questions, especially those pertaining to Death and mental health. I have been forced to ask these questions and, after many years and many changed answers to them, have started to become more consistent in my answers to them – this is telling me that the 'core' of my Self is happy with the direction I'm going in with these answers. Your answers will change, sometimes dramatically. Hell, for a while there I was a ideological communist! You ebb and flow. At the start the swings are big, and towards the end, they tighten up and you end up just swinging around more or less the same conclusion. That's the one you run with.

I've met people, having come home to Ireland after 4 years, who have never been outside their comfort zone and who not only don't have their answers and not only haven't asked the questions, but don't even know that the questions exist. It is for people like this that I worry, because one day they'll realise that the questions do exist and they'll need to find answers. The problem with that is that they may already have made commitments, and that's where problems happen like divorces, mid life crises etc…

- Ah, mid-life crises, a topic of interest for me. I look at midlife crises and I conclude that they are mis-named. Midlife crises, as we call them, are actually no such thing. The worst mid life crises that I have seen and heard of have happened to people who have well and truly had their shit together. Very successful in career etc. If anything, they were on a roll when the crisis happened! So how did it happen? The thing is, the crisis didn't happen when we say it happened – at 55 or whatever. The crisis we see is just a midlife output of the *actual* crisis, which happened 20 odd years before when they were in the Search Phase. If we see someone our age leave the Search Act nice and early and move into Act 2, we often assume they are 'ahead' of the pack. In actual fact, it is that very thing that can lead to the crisis down the road. Complete your search comprehensively. Get to know yourself, set up a life for that person – a career and partner and hobbies that actually suit them – and you have an excellent chance of being happy and being what your kids and everyone else will want you to be. Skip the search or take the easy road, and a midlife crisis could await you..

Act 2 – Creation

Families, businesses, charities, friend groups, art;

Whatever it is, eventually most people reach a point when they decide they are ready to commit their lives to the creation of something.

Very important point: There is no age by which a person should have left the Search Act and entered the Creation Act. You hear too many people say 'By 30 I want to be here in my career, and married with 2.5 kids and have the mortgage paid off' or some other such nonsense. We have no control over when we enter and exit phases. I know people who spent 1 year in the Search Act and dived straight into the Creation Act at 22. I know others who made the same transition in their late thirties. Neither one of these is 'doing better' than the other. The only way you can mess up this transition is to rush it (discussed earlier).

At the very heart of Act 2 is commitment. The goal is to live a committed life. That's easy. The real trick is to live a committed life that you are actually happy to commit to – that's the hard part. That's where a thorough search comes in.

The transition to Act 2 can be a very trying time for people. They freak out. They're behind on their 'This is where I'll be by 30' vision and they start to worry. Don't. There's no such thing as 'what a 30 year old should be'. I know 30 year olds who run multi-million dollar businesses. I also know 30 years olds who are currently trying to 'find themselves' in South America. Neither of these is necessarily better than the other. Everyone is just on their own path, trying to find a life they can commit to. If you are in that transition phase, don't freak out. It should be smooth. Seamless. If it's not, don't force it. Stay in the search mindset just a little longer and one day you'll wake up in a committed life without even realising that you've successfully made that transition. That's the dream: a seamless transition. If the transition is stressful or clunky or requires too dramatic a 'step up', I suggest you keep searching, as you might well be trying to step up into a life that, for now, belongs to someone else.

The idea of a 'committed life' sounds pretty bloody scary doesn't it? But if you're doing it right, it really shouldn't. I mean, picture the 'personal life' side of it. Do you think grooms in successful marriages are up on the altar thinking 'Oh Jesus I can't believe I have to spend the rest of my frickin life with this woman?' No! The ones in successful marriages can't wait to dive into that commitment and give it their all. Same goes for career. If you're thinking 'Oh God how am I gonna get through this', you're signing up for a job/relationship/commitment that's meant for someone else. The ones meant for you won't invoke that reaction. If something is meant for you it will fit smoothly.

If anything, it's really exciting. I think it's a primal urge to use one's life to create, whether that means creating a family, a business or any other type of legacy. I just think it's a natural inclination. It certainly excites and drives me more than anything else. It should be something that you look forward to and are not daunted by. If you commit to the things you're meant to commit to, you'll build fantastic things and have a great time doing it. If you try to force yourself to build things that are meant for someone else, you'll probably screw it up, get beaten by the person who was actually meant to do it, and have a miserable time in the process.

Your call.

You can probably see the recurring theme here: it is our insistence on living lives that we *think* we should rather than lives we *feel* we should that leads us to unhappiness.

Change that and the world is yours.

Looking for an easy way to summarise the 2 Acts? Simple.
Act 1- Choose your brush.
Act 2 – Paint your masterpiece.

Who Dressed You this Morning?

No, I'm not asking who you woke up this morning, and I'm not asking if your mom is the one who buttons up your shirt and does your tie.

What I'm talking about is something else entirely. You see, what I have noticed throughout my life to date – and I know that everybody else shares this, which is why I'm not shy admitting it – is that there are certain people in our lives who have a place in our minds. When we make decisions, the judgement that we expect these people to pass on these decisions is a considerable factor in them.

Take for example a fifteen-year-old boy. He's getting dressed in the morning. There are a lot of people influencing what he will wear that day: the cool kids at school, the girl he fancies, the teachers and school dress code, and, yes, probably his mom. While it may appear that he has full autonomy over what he wears every day, the reality is that by the time he has put his decision through these four or five filters, the choice is actually much more limited.

So that's the theory's framework, and that's just a boy getting dressed. But that same framework applies to many of us as young adults. Sure, in relation to what we wear to work or college or nights out, but also in relation to where we work, whether or not we do the accounting exams, whether or not we take a year out and go travelling, start a business, admit we are looking for a girlfriend, decide to quit drinking for a while...the list is endless. Just like that teenage boy, we too have people in our lives whose judgement of us matters enough to us for it to shape our decisions and, thus, our lives. I have had this, and while I'd like to say I'm pretty much out of it now, I'm sure there will be new people who will come into my life and play a similar role at some point. What I did to overcome this was simple but difficult:

1- I wrote a list of everyone who had a voice in my head and a say in my decisions.
2- I worked out why they did. What was it about them that gave them sufficient authority in my eyes to have input into how I shape my life.
3- I worked on the shortcoming in me – usually values-based – that conceded to that person's judgement, and I worked on that shortcoming.
4- I really focussed on making all of my decisions from inside me without any external interruption. I believe there is a little beacon way deep inside us that knows exactly what we want, and that there is a tunnel through which it sends those messages to our brain. The problem is that that tunnel is clogged with external inputs, other

people's voices etc. As we listen to that beacon more and let that message come all the way through, the tunnel clears and we can more easily know and do exactly what the deepest part of us wants.

You wouldn't let assholes live in your house; Why let them live in your head??

Love

'If you live without love you live not.'

Death taught me that.

That was the first time we met, when I originally had the cardiac arrest back on New Zealand in 2011. At that point, I had never loved. I was very cold hearted, in fact. When I woke up from the coma and slowly got to grips with what had happened, I felt strongly that if that were to be the end for me – if that was going to be as much as I was going to get out of this whole 'life' business – then I was getting a raw deal. There was something missing.

Now at this point you're probably expecting me to say that I sat up in my hospital bed and shouted out that love was the secret to happiness.

Not the case. <u>At that point I was still negotiating with the nurses to let me go and pee on my own instead of pissing into a pipe that they had feeding into my cock for the week that I'd been out</u>. Then I got out of hospital, drank like a fish and relentlessly chased girls for 3 years, and became, if anything, a strong proponent of the argument that love didn't actually exist at all.

But in time I learned. And I learned that love was in fact that missing ingredient. Now that I have had it, I feel like dying back then would have meant I'd never lived at all for not having experienced it, and I encourage every one of you to make yourselves open to its grasp as you see fit.

Because that is what love entails. You have to open yourself up to it. You have to allow it to take hold. It's very much like entrepreneurship, really. In both entrepreneurship and in love:

- You can only enjoy the ultimate reward if you expose yourself to the possibility of crashing and burning
- There are mediocre rewards for no risk, and indescribable rewards for high risk
- It takes real courage to do either one properly
- It will be both the most challenging and most rewarding thing you'll ever do
- You may have to try and fail and face a lot of pain before you're ready for the venture that is tailor made for you
- Neither journey is ever complete, and the learning never ends

So that is love, and to be fair, it gets a lot of air time. What doesn't get as much air time is that, while love is the ultimate energy (and in many cultures is revered as God), love also comes in many forms, the first and foremost of which is Self Love.

Self Love

Someone with strong self-love is very comfortable in their own skin, and very comfortable in their own company. These are sure signs of self-love. Self-love cannot be faked, and if faking of it is attempted, the only victim of the pretence is the pretender. Authentic self-love is the result of very honest self-reflection. The individual looks inward constantly, wondering how she can improve. She looks at her strengths and checks where she has used them well and where she could use them more. She looks at her weaknesses. She starts by forgiving herself for these weaknesses because weaknesses are as much a part of being a human as are lungs and a heart. She looks not just at how she can improve on these weaknesses, but also at how she can use them to her advantage. She is under no illusion that she is perfect, and she loves her imperfections because they are as much a part of her as anything else.

Self-Love has to be step 1 because one's love for one's self has no external influences. She approves of herself. She reports to herself. She seeks to make herself proud of herself. The approval, pride and love of others come after this, and add icing to that cake, of course, but the foundation of all love is self-love. After all, why should someone else love and approve of you if you do not love and approve of yourself? This self-love and self-approval are what provide her with the courage and strength of will to go against the grain, stand out from the crowd, and be disruptive in society. She approves of their own actions, so the disapproval of others has no effect. Of course, she listens to the reasons people give for their disapproval, for that provides her with information, but she processes that in her own way and, if she continues to approve of herself, she continues on her course.

Good v Great

Winston Churchill once said that 'Good and Great are rarely the same man'.
Let's explore that...

What I initially thought he meant was that great men (and women) were often
required to do things that weren't considered good in order to achieve a desired
outcome. Simple as that. But I've done some thinking, and I've arrived at the
conclusion that, really, good people and great people aren't actually measured on
the same scale.

Good people are measured by societal standards. Good job, good money, good
morals, good behaviour, good family. Good good good.

It's good to be good.

But it's not great.

You see, people who strive to be good can only ever be good. They can never be
great. No great person, on the other hand, ever strived to be good, because if you
strive to be good then good is the best you can be. You can be good or you can be
bad. Or, on the other scale, you can be great or you can be tragic. There's no
middle ground here, and the line between great and tragic is particularly thin.

People who strive to be good play it safe. People who strive to be great do not.
Greatness cuts through. Greatness challenges. Greatness disrupts and goes against
the trend. Greatness demands that you play uncomfortably big hands, and usually
require significant loss before any gain is even in sight.

Good watches his step. Great blazes ahead. Good follows the crowd. Great follows
her heart. Good waits for a lift. Great starts walking. Nobody has a problem with
Good. Great collects detractors and admirers in equal proportions. Good is in the
stands, watching and commentating. Great is on the field, toiling and bleeding.
Great tries and fails. Good never tries.

Good talks about Great, for better or worse. Great doesn't know Good exists.
Good envies Great. Great envies no one.

The only people who ever get to be great are the ones who risked being tragic.
Mandela might never made it out of jail. Ghandi too. Jobs might have gone
bankrupt. Obama might have been assassinated by white extremists. All of these
people that we consider to have achieved great things – every single one of them

– could just as easily ended up being deemed a tragedy story, and for every one that we hold up on a pedestal, there are 100 just like them whom fortune didn't favour, who are indeed considered tragedies.

There is nothing wrong with Good. Good is safe. Good pays the bills and has weekends off. Good can relax. Good has many perks. Just don't expect Great for the price of Good. That doesn't exist.

Habits & Choices

Aristotle said 'We are what we repeatedly do. Success is therefore not an act but a habit'.

Couldn't agree more. I look at habits as an algorithm, where *you* are both the input and the output. You go in, you perform whatever habits you have in place, and a different version of you comes out the other side. If you have a drinking habit, a fatter, unhealthier you with less brain cells comes out. If you have a smoking habit, a version of you with lung cancer comes out. If you have a gym habit, a fitter version of you comes out. If you have a reading habit, a wiser version of you comes out the other side.

Where I got my habits from is a vision of the version of myself that I wanted to be. I got the vision clear in my head, saw the difference between that guy and me, and put the right habit algorithm in the middle. It makes for a really hard month as you introduce these habits. You miss some days and the days you don't miss, you often wish you did. But after that month, the habits settle in and, by the time another 3 months has passed, you'll struggle to get by without the practice of these new habits. Habits are the infrastructure that your day and your life is built around, so you want them to be strong, positive habits, not unhealthy ones that will hold you back.

Habits are also a valuable currency in a little bank you have. That bank takes two currencies, the other of which is choices. Good habits and good choices are deposits in the bank, while bad habits and choices are withdrawals. Let's take eating habits as an example.
If your breakfast habit is to have a bowl of Coco Pops and a can of coke every morning, you are making daily withdrawals. If you are going out on the piss two nights a week, that's two major withdrawals, and if you're like I used to be and insist on having a burrito and tub of Ben & Jerry's every time you're hungover, then that's two more large withdrawals.

If you have porridge every morning, on the other hand, and a healthy salad lunch and go to yoga or the gym every day, you are just making deposit after deposit and your 'bank balance' is shooting up.

As with any bank balance, the idea is to never go below zero, for that would be running into a deficit (poor health and energy, in this case). At the same time, there's no point in being the richest person in the graveyard either – we have to live a little! If you have healthy habits all week, you can afford to have that Full Irish or few pints on the weekend. If that's what allows you to switch off and gear up for another week of solid deposits, then go for it. If you spend the week making withdrawals though, then making more on the weekend is like going shopping on an overdue credit card, you just can't afford it.

With good habits you can afford bad choices.

Our habits define us. If we have normal habits, we will achieve a normal outcome, If we have extreme habits, we will have an extreme outcome. So if you want to be extremely successful, don't expect to get there if you have the same comfortable, normal habits as everyone around you. The algorithm doesn't work that way. Extreme output doesn't follow average input. Likewise, if you have extremely bad habits, don't expect a normal outcome. If you drink or smoke a lot or are particularly lazy at work, don't expect to have a normal life. You won't. You'll struggle health wise, financially, and in any other way that your inputs are below par.

There's something else important about habits that I think you already know. We don't feel them. We grow numb to them. If you have a habit of getting up at 5am, that will be tough for the first month. But after a while, you get used to it and you don't even notice it after a while. Switching from Coco Pops to porridge will be horrible for the first month. But after a while, you'll forget what it was even like to have Coco Pops every morning and you'll feel the same about the porridge as you used to feel about the Coco Pops, only the porridge will be serving you well. By that token, there's really no point in having bad habits, because good or bad, we grow numb to them. We stop tasting the sweetness in the Coco Pops and stop tasting the blandness in the porridge. Everything just becomes 'normal', so why not create a normal that's serves you rather than one that holds you back?

Exercise:

What habits do you have that hold you back?
What habits do you have that propel you?
What habits do you not have that you would benefit from introducing?

Health & Happiness

Sticking with the health theme for a minute; There is a strong connection between happiness and health, and it goes both ways. By doing things that make you happy, you will improve your health (provided those things that make you happy aren't blatantly unhealthy). Inversely, then, being physically healthy gives you a much better chance of being happy. Why? Because our bodies are extremely complex physiological systems, where our physical health has a strong impact on the chemicals that control our emotions. To be honest, I kind of knew this was true – it just made sense to me. But I had no idea how true it is:

Serotonin is known as the Happiness Hormone. 95% of our serotonin is produced in our gut.
Dopamine, our 'reward hormone', is also produced almost exclusively in our gut, as is the chemical responsible for our ability to deal with stress.

This is one that Death didn't need to tell us because Science already has: real happiness requires the chemical platform of good health. If you lack that, no matter how good your life might be, you are not chemically wired to experience the emotional heights that humans are supposed to. You lack the biological infrastructure required to feel good.

What's one thing you could do to make yourself healthier?

Courage

When we think about Death, we get uncomfortable. I really think it's worth reflecting on why this is so. Everyone's reason will be different. Before Death entered my life at age 18, I actually can't remember how I felt about it. Come to think of it, I don't think I ever even thought about it; I was an 18 year who felt totally invincible; Why would Death even cross my mind? That seems alien to me now. I literally can't imagine what it would be like to go a few days without thinking about Death.

The reason I have found the aftermath of my interactions so tough is often because of the thinking and course corrections required. Death is like the friend who double dares and triple dares you to do the crazy shit that scares the hell out of you!

"Quit your job – I dare ya, I dare ya!"
"Go travelling alone – I dare ya, I dare ya!"
"Write a book and tell everyone about it – I dare ya, I dare ya!"
"Start a business no matter who tells you not to – I dare ya, I dare ya!"

I mean, these were all things I wanted to do deep down, but there was just this huge mental barrier in my head that was stopping me from doing them. I was telling myself that the timing wasn't right, my surroundings and circumstances at that particular time weren't right for it, I was very comfortable in my job and life at that time and I didn't want to disrupt that etc...all of which might have been in some way true.

But Death doesn't think like that. If Death had a job title, it would be something like 'Life Renovation Expert'.
It's Death's job to go into the building of your life and rip it to the ground. Everything. The walls that shape your very world, the floors that provide you with security underfoot, the luxuries and toys you paid for and love, even some of the people that live in your house. He tears everything down until there is nothing left but that foundation.
Then he turns around and he says 'Forget everything you knew about your life and the world around you. The only thing you have in common with who you have been to date is your height and the colour of your hair. Build the fucking thing the way you want it from now, not the way someone else wants you to have it and not the way you used to want it; *the way you want it now*. Different materials, different shape, different people, different everything. I'm coming back soon but I'm not telling you when. Good Luck."

This is where courage comes in. It takes courage to break your cycle of thinking, disengage with the life you're used to living in and, ideally, even forget what that was like.

It then takes courage to design the life you really want. Really, that exploration of yourself takes a lot of courage. It's very difficult and very arduous and, despite your best intentions, you'll constantly look back on how good and nice your old life was, and that's *torture*. It takes courage to go through that, seeing clearly all the best bits from your past while not even knowing what the future looks like yet. All you can see is what you've walked away from.

Finally then, it takes courage to actually go after the life you've thought up. It takes courage even telling people the vision for that, because, realistically, it's probably going to be pretty awesome. People won't cope well with that, partly because they lack the courage to do a renovation on their own lives and they don't want to see you succeed, and partly because they genuinely have your best interests at heart and they're worried about you striving for Great and ending in Tragedy. It takes courage to keep going there, and it takes courage to distance yourself from the people in that first bracket, because you might frankly be surprised by some of the faces you see there.

It all takes incredible courage, but that's the price for living the life you want. If you're reading this, you're probably in the top 1% wealthiest people in the world. The opportunities available to you in this life are limitless. Literally, limitless. If you're reading this you're also probably under 35. Think about how different the world is now to when you were a kid. Think about how fast it's evolved. Now think about where it will be in another 20 or 30 years. You'll still be fully active by then. What could you possibly not achieve at that point??

Courage is at the centre of everything. It takes courage to change, it takes courage to really grow, it takes courage to try, it takes courage to love, and expose yourself to heartbreak. Courage is at the centre of all great things, and its absence is at the centre of all mediocrity.

Drugs

Death has taught me that our most valuable asset is time and, the same way we are reluctant to waste and squander money with no reward, so too should we be reluctant to squander our time.

What does wasted time vs time well spent look like? Well, that is specific to each one of us depending on our values and goals. But for simplicity's sake, let's just say that wasted time is time spent being preventably miserable or unproductive and time well spent is time spent being happy or productive.

So now we're talking about happiness and misery. Where do each of them come from? That's the magic question, isn't it? There is no golden answer, because its different, again, for each of us. But there is some pretty strong suggestive evidence we can look at:

When you get really drunk, you have a hangover the next day. Hangovers suck. Here's how I look at this one – it's a bit nerdy but it makes sense:

We generally value having a great weekend over having a great Friday night. We want to have as close to a 10/10 weekend as possible.
The weekend is made up of hours.
Let's say you spend 7 hours out on a Friday night, and 17 hours awake on a Saturday.
If you get really drunk on Friday, you'll have 8 fantastic hours, each a 9/10. Then on Saturday, you'll have 17 average hours – each a 5/10. Over all, you have 157 'enjoyment points' over Friday and Saturday (9x8+17x5)

Say you don't drink when you go out. It won't be as fun, but it will still be fun. Let's say it's 7/10 fun (it's definitely higher but let's stretch the example). The next day, then, you feel fresh and you can go hiking, swimming, running, whatever. You have a great Saturday. 9/10. You end that Friday/Saturday combo with 209 enjoyment points - a significantly better weekend. Add to that the fact that you save a lot of money, and all of a sudden this whole 'not getting drunk' idea makes a lot of sense!

Delving in to the harder drugs, then, we use the same logic but on a different level. Instead of talking about one-day hangovers, we're talking more about long term cerebral health. Simply put, hard drugs like cocaine, ecstasy and even, to a lesser extent, marijuana, put a strain on your brains' production of rewarding neurotransmitters like dopamine, exhausting it and its ability to produce these transmitters in everyday life. Basically, your brain gets used to such high doses of dopamine from cocaine that it simply becomes numb to the lower, but more frequent, dopamine triggers offered by natural, everyday life. End result: you get high as a kite and have a great time on coke but become chronically bored by life when you are not on it. If you ever spend time with someone who does a lot of coke, they're generally really boring and low, because life doesn't excite them anymore. The things that excite us and our lives don't give them a dose of dopamine strong enough for them to feel it.

So, back to our numbers game, you get 100 nights out on coke and they're all 10/10 (yep, just one point above the rest because you can't get above 10/10), and you lose enjoyment points on every other hour of your life thereafter. Weed: similar effect: awful for mental health and can really accelerate the degradation of your brain (early alzheimers, psychosis, schizophrenia all result). It just doesn't make sense as a thing to do. Then again, life doesn't have to make logical sense, and you might not have any interest in being happy in the long run, having a functioning brain or being able to talk to your grandchildren, in which case snort and smoke away. This is just one way of presenting the topic and might be different to how you've looked at it before.

Time is the asset, and I want to get as much out of all of it, not just some of it, as I possibly can. I want to be consistently happy in life. As far as I know, so does every human on earth. 'Consistent Happiness', as the name suggests, requires consistency. How am I going to achieve consistency if I expose my mind to the enormous chemical swings brought on by drug use? Regarding happiness, then – the other half of the goal – refer back to the above regarding dopamine depletion. If someone tells me they want to be happy and then does a load of drugs, I jump to one of two conclusions:

1- They don't actually want to be happy because drugs are proven both scientifically and anecdotally to have the opposite long-term effect, or
2- They do want to be happy but they're either too weak to say no or too stupid to realise that drug use + long term, consistent happiness do not equate.

It's totally their decision and it's got nothing to do with me, I'm just telling you the conclusions that I draw.
Each to their own!

Mental Diet

Drugs are not the only thing to pollute the mind.

People talk a lot today about health and exercise and what foods to eat, etc. They understand that putting bad food into your body will make your body unwell either immediately or in the long run. On the contrary, putting good food in as consistently as possible can make your body feel and look great, and enable you to enjoy all of the benefits and positive side-effects of that.

What people are less cognisant of is the fact that the exact same principle applies to the mind. Just as you need to maintain a healthy bodily diet, you also need to maintain a healthy mental diet. What is your mind consuming, and how can you improve that diet?

While your body needs to avoid - habitually - chocolate, cigarettes, alcohol, ice-cream etc, here are a list of things that your mind needs to avoid, but sometimes might crave:

- People you follow on social media that have a poor impact on your self-perception. Whether its ripped guys or 'Professional Arses' on Instagram, or a Twitter account that tells you that you're living wrong, you need to cut this out of your diet. This is mental abuse the same way that polishing off a tub of Ben & Jerrys is (albeit a delicious form of-) physical abuse. Sure, a certain amount of it can be inspiring, but most people consume far more than that and it affects them psychologically on levels they don't even know.
- Friends who complain or belittle you. Complainers are like burst fire hydrants of negativity. They just spray it on everyone who is walking by. If you saw a fire hydrant on a footpath, you would keep a wide berth. Do the same with complainers and inconsiderate people.
- People with alcohol or substance abuse issues. Anyone who has dealt with this shit will know how toxic it is. It is impossible to have substance abuse in your life either directly or indirectly, and also enjoy positive mental health simultaneously.
- Negative narratives (more on that in next chapter)
- Wasteful TV. TV is like crisps. Lovely to crunch on but have no nutrition. Diagnosis – enjoy as a weekend snack but not as a dietary habit. (If you're in Ireland, I recommend Ripples ;-))

There are a thousand others. I suggest creating a list of all the things and people that your mind regularly consumes. Is there a person that you always walk away from feeling refreshed and happy, or laughing with? Schedule more time with her. Is there a person that drags you down or stresses you out? Schedule less time with that person. Is there an activity you do that consistently puts you in a good headspace? Build a habit around it. This stuff sounds obvious, I know, but if you're anything like me, you will see that you are very far away from actually optimising your consumption of these things.

Nothing in life is more valuable than a positive mindset and happy heart. We should all be doing more to achieve these things.

The Power of Narrative

Last year, in the depths of Post Traumatic Stress Disorder, I learned that narrative was the single biggest driver of my outlook, my behaviour and, in several ways, my life.

That's right: narrative. Story. And I don't mean the external narrative that you create about your life and making that as interesting as possible, as the old cliché goes. I'm talking about the many loud, discrete, and sometimes even subconscious narratives that float our own heads, never to be repeated aloud.

"I can't talk to boys because they'll see my acne and think it's ridiculous'
'I can't go out without drinking because people will think I'm not a badass'
'I really want to ask for that promotion but if the boss says no I'll look stupid'

There are hundreds of them, maybe thousands. Some, like those listed above, are common to many people, while others are unique. One of the best things I have ever done for myself was related to this. First, I have to give you the background:

It was July 2017 and I had been suffering from PTSD for 6 months at this point. Narratives had had a very serious impact on my mental health:

- I had become a hermit. I never went out, because I thought that if I did, I would never exude the energy and charisma that I had before my shock in January, and I thought people would no longer enjoy my company, or that they would see the vulnerability in me when they saw me. Seriously damaging, as it meant I never saw my friends, never went out, and experienced some level of social anxiety on the rare occasions that I did.
- I had stopped exercising. Now, I had also given up eating meat, drinking alcohol and eating basically anything other than fruit and veg, so I actually lost weight, but the longer I went on telling myself that exercise was bad for my heart, the more afraid of it I became. I now exercise too little and haven't run in almost two years, purely because I am afraid to.
- I used to have about 3 nightmares a week and a mini panic attack most days. In every nightmare, my heart went into failure and I work up screaming, and in every panic attack I would suddenly jump to the conclusion that I was about to enter cardiac arrest. This stopped me walking to and from work, walking up a stairs, and even had me wait for an Uber lying on my back on a public footpath, because I was

afraid to stay standing. There was absolutely nothing wrong with my heart at any of these times. All narrative.

The best thing I ever did for myself came when I decided that enough was enough with all this. I booked a holiday on my own up to the Whitsunday Islands in northern Australia. I sat in a café there and wrote a list of everything I had become afraid of. I then wrote a list of challenges for myself for that week in order to overcome those fears.

I'd become afraid of socialising, so I approached a group every night in a restaurant and asked them if I could join them. Weird, scary and very beneficial (and fun!)

I had become afraid of talking to girls because I had lost all confidence, so I tried to chat up one a day.

I had become very afraid of water, so I went on a snorkelling trip out on the Great Barrier Reef. I nearly had a genuine heart attack when I first looked down and saw how deep it was – I had been freaking out in swimming pools for the previous 7 months – but I stayed in for an hour and my fear subsided.

I had become afraid of walking long distances on my own, so I went for morning and evening walks.

I was afraid to quit Google. I knew I didn't like it there, but I had become afraid to trust my gut and go with my heart. I arrived back in Sydney from the trip on Sunday, and I went in on Monday morning and quit, having no idea what lay ahead for me.

All of these things petrified me. They really shouldn't have, but I had subconsciously crafted narratives in my head – like 'if you walk up these stairs, you'll die' – that prevented me from doing the most basic of things.

Narratives like these but maybe less extreme could be – and probably are – affecting your life on some level too. I recommend you do what is now my favourite exercise for myself:

Write out 3 lists of narratives:
1- Narratives you tell yourself that hold you back
2- Narratives you tell yourself that drive you forward
3- Narratives you don't tell yourself but that you could benefit from if you did

I have done this several times now and I find it extremely powerful. I uncover narratives that I didn't know I had. I uncover how and why I am holding myself back in certain parts of my life, and I uncover some of the most powerful tools I need to elevate myself to the next level up in all areas. I hope it helps you to do the same.

Act from positive emotions

Often times, when the word "Death' comes up, the word 'regret' isn't behind. When the word 'regret' is raised, then, we start to think about its two main sources: things we have done and things we haven't done.

There's a hard and fast rule we can apply here that will pretty much protect us against any regret stemming from that first source. That rule is to *only act from positive emotions.*

Now that's a lot easier said than done. We've all, on many occasions, done things driven by negative emotions like anger, spite, disappointment etc. We shouldn't feel bad about having those emotions, or even about having done those things. They're both totally human and perfectly natural.

But here's what I realised: Emotions are transient, while actions last forever. If you are angry, that will pass, and eventually you will no longer be angry. If you are angry and you act out of that anger, that action will be permanent and, as circumstances change, you may well live to regret it. Disappointment, hatred etc, same thing. On the other hand, if you are happy, joyous etc; While your emotions will eventually subside just like negative ones would, you are much less likely to regret any actions you commit while under their influence.

If half of your regret comes from things you have done, you may well be able to halve the amount of regret you feel by always waiting for negative emotions to subside before acting!

The first step to success

I don't think being successful is easy by any stretch of the imagination, but I sure as hell don't think it is as hard as people make it out to be. I think there are many people who have the capability to do everything that success requires – hard work, perseverance, consistent focus etc – who don't end up being successful, not because they fall at one of the hurdles, but because they don't even make it to the track.

The first step to being successful - at absolutely anything at all – is defining success. *That*'s the hardest part. *That's* where we all fall short.
As someone who is more guilty of this than anyone – I have moved the goalposts for myself more times than I care to admit – I have learned through experience that finding a sustainable definition of what success means to you is a very, very difficult thing to do.

You will never be successful if you live to serve someone else's value set. Why not? Because even if you ace that value set and 'win that game', it won't feel like success because it's not a part of you, it's a part of them. It wasn't your game to play. Accomplishing something that someone else values but you don't, and not feeling great about it afterwards? That doesn't sound like success to me...

So how do you find your values? Well that ties back in to Act 1 – The Search.

Our Hidden Superpower

I've realised recently that one of the things that we humans have the most control over, in our lives, is how the people around us feel. Every person has a thousand different emotions that they might feel at any given time: empowered, confident, proud, ashamed, loved, alone, afraid, unappreciated...the list goes on. And each of us has, at one point in our lives, felt each of these emotions. While we don't necessarily always have power over which one of these *we* feel at a given point, we do in fact have more power over how the people around us feel. That power is exercised through what we say and what we do.

If you were sitting next to me, we could chit chat and both remain at an emotional neutral. You could say something really cruel to me and discourage me, make me feel ashamed, or sad. Alternatively, you could say something really encouraging, or complementary, or positive, and that would uplift me.
There are 3 ways I feel walking away from that meeting – down, neutral, or up – and the biggest influence on that is the decision you make as to what to do, what body language to use, and, of course, what you choose to say.
It's a strange thing, right? I'm not saying you're responsible for my overall happiness and vice versa. That has to be up to the individual. I'm saying that you have a huge input into how I feel at any given point, and I'm encouraging you to use that power often, and for the better.
It can be weird giving compliments, or uncomfortable. We rarely want to give complements to people who have what we want, because of our own insecurity over the fact that they have it and we don't. Try to move past that. We also find it awkward to give complements, particularly in late teens or early twenties. It's just not considered cool to show your hand like that. Let me just guarantee you that your definition of what is 'cool' is about to dramatically change in the next few years, and there is a very strong negative correlation between efforts to be cool in your early twenties and success in your later twenties. Lose that childish priority now, start being a leader in making the people around you feel great, and you will find yourself in a much better position because of it.

My favourite quote I have ever heard, from G.K Chesterton:

"The great man is the man who makes every man feel great"

Community & Support

It is anecdotally proven that regular company, community and a support network are very important to health. The health of those who have these things benefits from them, and the health of those who do not have them suffers as a result.

When you read that information, it is natural that the first thing you wonder is 'do I have this in my life?'. An excellent second question might be 'in whose life do I play this role, and am I doing as good a job as I can for them?'

Living in a world full of too many people and not enough humans, an outstanding way to make a difference is to welcome a person into a community and give them that community and that support that we all crave. It is not a personal choice. It is not a matter of introverts vs extroverts. It is a feature designed into humans. We need community. It is at the heart of our highest and lowest feelings. The highest – love and adoration – require others, and the lowest – shame and loneliness – are derived from either the presence (or lack thereof) of others.
That is a powerful thing to be aware of.

Investments

Imagine Tesco paid a dividend last week, and all the shareholders got cheques in the mail. I wasn't a shareholder, but I started to complain that I didn't get a cheque.

That'd be illogical, right? How would I get a dividend if I didn't invest? I had no right to a dividend and no reason to expect one.
I'm sure you'll agree.
But for some reason, while you might agree with that, you might also be guilty of the exact same illogical expectations yourself, in other areas of your life.
In order to prevent ourselves from being disappointed by outcomes that we weren't hoping for – not getting the promotion, not getting the girl/boy or whatever else we were aspiring to - we need to draw a clear line between our input and our desired output. You don't train for a marathon by thinking about treadmills. You have to consistently and relentlessly go for runs, pushing yourself on almost every one of them. That approach is what gets you marathon fit, what gets you promoted, and what gets you almost anything else worth chasing in this life.

A great exercise that I run through in my workshops is this:

1) Write down your current investment portfolio of your time and energy. You have 168 hours in a week. How do you invest / spend them? (Difference between investing time and spending it is that spending brings instant gratification, investing brings delayed gratification)

2) Write down your one-year vision for yourself in the areas that matter: Health, Career, Relationships, Skills & Hobbies, Financial, Adventures. What does 'You in One Year' look like in these areas? What are they doing? What have they done in the meantime? What new skills do they have? Where are they living, working etc?

3) Write down the changes that need to be made to your investment strategy in order to make that vision a reality. It is likely that some changes will be needed, especially when you remember that a year is a very short space of time!

I often feel sorry for kids who are in circumstances that they don't like, because there's nothing they can do about it. However, I never feel sorry for adults in this position, because adults – particularly those reading this book – have full authority over their circumstances, and only need courage and a strategy to change them.

Health

One investment we see lots of people our age make, is into their bodies. There are girls for whom life is just one, drawn out arse workout, and there are guys who walk around with a downright inconvenient amount of muscle padded onto themselves.

I think this is crazy for three reasons.

1) **The investment:** If you are a gym junkie, take a minute to think about the numbers around that habit. Not money, time (unless supplements etc are breaking your bank). Let's say you spend 1hr in the gym a day, which is probably low for you guys. You probably spend a half hour getting ready, having pre-workout etc. You probably spend 1.5 hours doing meal prep and cooking the 5,000 calories you have concluded you need in order to sustain your desired weight. You are placing a huge amount of time into this habit. Not the 1 hour/day you're spending in the gym, but 3.5 hours on the whole package. I had a friend complaining about this to me recently. He started a daily 1hr gym habit, got serious about it, and all of a sudden was losing 4 hours in the day. That's about 25 hours / week! That's more than what I spent writing this book in a week. The average full-time job in France is 35 hours/ week. You getting jacked is almost like a full-time job, and you don't get paid for it? That's crazy.

2) **The Return:** Now for girls, I can't really comment. I think being fit is great but I feel for the girls who feel the pressure to make it their whole life, get surgeries etc. I wish they all knew that just being who they are and comfortable with their imperfections – which we all have – is more than enough. For boys, it gets a little bit funnier to me. I wonder, when I see a guy walking down the street who is shaped like a cube - equal height, width and thickness – what that person is going to do with that body. He has designed himself to be able to squat a car. When is he going to need to do that? Who is going to value that? The thousand-hour investment he made in acquiring that ability to squat half a ton; when is that investment going to pay a dividend? Would that time not have been more wisely invested in his mind, which will navigate him through the world, dictate his career, personal life and outlook? Would that not be a much, much more fruitful investment than anything else? I'm not

mocking them. I'm sure they have their reasons. I just find it strange and illogical.

I also feel compelled to warn these guys about their influences here. Dwayne 'The Rock' Johnson must be the most famous jacked guy on the planet. If you follow him on Instagram, he is very entertaining and very inspiring, because he works extremely hard. Here's the problem: We see him work hard – almost always in the gym – and that then comes to represent to us what 'working hard' means – going to the gym. The disconnect lies in the fact that he gets paid for that. He is not successful because of his acting ability. He is successful because he is built, quite literally, like a silverback guerrilla, yet he is a human. He is makes $60 million a year because he is a guerrilla-shaped human. He is *the* guerrilla-shaped human. That's his job. If he stops doing it, he'll stop earning money.
But he is one of about 5 guys in the world for whom that is true. For everyone else – including you and me – our bodies are very unlikely to be the thing to define our place in society and in the world, or to make us money. They are unlikely to be at the centre of any success we have. The hard part for us is identifying what is (hint – it's squishy and sits in your skull) and invest in that instead. Still follow the Rock, learn from his work rate, but acknowledge the fact that what the gym represents for him, is represented by something entirely different for you and I.

3)   **The Health:** I used to be jacked. I used to take creatine twice a day and protein about 3 times. I was 117kg with very little fat. Then I died, came back, and that was no longer a priority, as it was not a healthy way for me to be living. Now I'm a dainty 100 kg, eat mostly vegetables, and don't drink. Why? Because what I want from my body has changed. I used to want it to smash into things and win the collision, and now I want it to survive for 100 years without as few health troubles as possible.
Here's my point. Being reasonably muscular can look really good (go too far and you look insecure and image-obsessed). It can be really healthy. With most of the cases I see, though, it's not healthy. The diets are great for muscle growth and bad for internal health. That's problem 1; some of these guys will have serious heart, kidney and liver issues way earlier than they should. Problem 2 is that, even if the physical health stuff isn't an issue, the mental health side is really imbalanced. Being that obsessed with how your body is shaped – such a surface and superficial thing – is not healthy for a person's growth. I know a lot of it is insecurity-driven. I'm not looking down on that, because we all have insecurities, and this is just your one. Mine

is something different and the next person's is different again. I guess I just want to say that you shouldn't let your insecurity take such hold of your life and your health and your time. As you move into your late twenties, you'll see people's values change. The girl who once wanted a big, ripped guy will now want a smart, nice guy with an interesting mind, and that's the direction she - and her desires - will keep moving in.

To the girls, same thing; guys will care less and less about whatever little shortcoming that you have that you think is holding you back, and they'll care more about what's inside. Corny, but true. Plan for that. Don't trip yourself up by going on this path of image obsession, where you will spend your life just trying to keep up with your past self or those around you. Guys objectify girls too much, that's totally true and that needs to change. But girls objectify themselves even more, and if I'm honest, that breaks my heart even more.

Dream Life

Imagine your dream life.
Now colour it in. What are all the details? What do you do every day?
My answer to this used to be the usual young guys' answer – big house, fast cars, no work, hot girls...you know the drill.
When I think about what it would actually be like to live that life, spending every day out on a boat, waking up whenever I want, having no troubles etc and no job, I get a little bit sad. I get sad, not because I want that life and I don't have it, but because that's the life I tell myself I am aspiring to, yet when I imagine actually living it, I imagine myself getting very bored very quickly.
I imagine myself wanting job – a reason to wake up in the morning; Something to get up for; Something to challenge me, grow me and absorb me, giving me an opportunity to show the world what I have to offer, while also finding that out for myself.
I think about the models and all that stuff, and I get sad imagining a life where the people around you are there because of how they look and what you have, rather than what either of you are really like inside. I get sad at the thought of being surrounded by people who don't care about me and I don't care about them, rather than someone who, while they might drive you crazy now and then and vice versa, is genuinely in your corner in all parts of life just as you are in theirs.

My point is this: We often dream about escaping the day to day lives that we live. The jobs, the stress, the ups and downs in a relationship, the absence of all of the flashy shit that we see online. But the reality is, for most of us, that if we were in that life, the only thing we would crave would be the ups and downs of day to day life. Why? Because that is what makes us human. Humans are extremely complex, interdependent creatures. We are stimulated in millions of invisible but crucial ways every single day in our lives, and it is that stimulation that keeps us going, keeps us driven, unpredictable and growing. If we took away the catalysts for those millions of stimulants – our jobs, our housemates, our friends and girlfriends who make us laugh, make us think, drive us mad and experience life with us, then we would all of a sudden be very bored and wouldn't understand why. This would make us sad, confused, and disillusioned with life, success, and what they were both supposed to mean.

That is why, for me, that vision is gone. Now, success to me looks like being positively stimulated by- and appreciative of – everyday life and the people and places in it. It's not about being a hedge fund manager, an NBA star or a pro soccer player. Sure, those jobs are cool and those guys are very lucky. But the reason athletes are lucky isn't the money, the fame etc. The human condition is exempt from all that.

What makes athletes lucky is that they achieve glory in moments. We don't. We achieve glory very gradually and inconspicuously, when one moment is never very different to the last. Athletes need to master the art of the binary outcome – they score or they miss; they win or they lose. Black or white. We, on the other hand, need to master the art of the grey – the unclear, unmeasured type of success. Listen to an athlete after a game that she's won. She'll tell you she feels amazing and victorious. Then listen to a couple who have lived in a successful marriage for 40 years, or a businessman who has created a thriving company; both of those groups will tell you that they don't really *feel* successful, that's it's still just a daily input for them.

When people talk about 'entering the real world', then, and the change that comes with that, I think this exact thing is the biggest change: the switch from a world where the outcomes are binary (pass or fail, win or lose, graduate or not) and people focus on the outcome, to a world where outcomes are non-binary, and the focus is on *input*. That's where the shock comes from, because it requires a rewiring of the mind. If you can execute on that rewiring, shift your focus towards consistent input, and acquire the skill of keeping steady among the inevitable ebb and flow and choppy waters that define modern life, then you will have as enjoyable and as rewarding existence as is possible. Yin and Yang. The reason Yin exists is because natures dictates that you will crave it once you've had enough Yang. That is life.

Looking back to an extent is good because you extract lessons and learnings
Looking forward is good because you see where you want to go and you get insights into your true values and your fears.
Looking at present is good because it means you don't miss the party.
Again: balance. Yin and Yang.

The Goalposts

Competition has come up a few times in this book. I recently had a very honest conversation with a friend of mine about this recently. He went to college in Trinity and I went to UCD. We were both always very ambitious. We spoke about how we were secretly really competitive with each other and with anyone else our age that we had heard of that was 'doing well' or 'going to do well'. We'd ask around about them, what they were up to, take an interest in what they were earning…all the usual petty shit. We were just competitive young guys. Totally natural.

Then, as we left college, things started to move around a bit. I was the highest earner out of college but then left for Google and took a $40k pay cut. I was no longer the highest earner. But then again, money had fallen in my priorities. There were people earning more than me, but the petty little voice inside my head would bitterly ask 'Yeah, but are they really happy?', or 'Yeah, but that's not an ethical job, how can they sleep at night?'. That was my insecure way of saying that the goal posts had moved for me.

My friend had the exact same experience, and it was amazing to have such an honest conversation about such an inherent and ugly flaw. We talked about it; about how the goal posts keep changing as life goes on and priorities and circumstances evolve. We concluded, at the end of it, that there were in fact no goal posts. My mentor had already told me this. When he did, I told him that it was easy for him to say that, since he had already made a lot of money – he was already on top of the hill. He responded to this - in that annoyingly Zen manner of his - 'Mark, there is no hill'.

What's the takeaway here? I guess it's that there is no point in competing with those around us. We're running different races. We're playing different sports. You decide what your goal posts are. The less generic the goal posts you choose (ie, the more specific they are to you), the better. Compete with what you know you are capable of. Don't compete with anyone else around you. That will worsen relationships, create unwanted and unproductive noise in your head, and eat into your happiness and your ability to endure the day to day ebb and flow of life.

A second takeaway is that there are no goalposts. There is no such thing as 'having made it'. 'To have made it' is to be in the oasis, and the oasis is an illusion. When you finally make it to where you originally saw the oasis, you will find that the oasis is in fact not there, and that it is just as far away from you now as it had been when you started out. That is life. That is the human condition.

Where is this relevant? Mainly in goal setting. Most of us 'laundry list' our goals – we create a list of things we want to accomplish or do by a certain time, and we tick them off as we do them. We work down the list.

I'm trying to move away from this. Sure, I still have my goals and things I want to do that once I do, will be done. But more important are the goals about which that seemingly obvious statement isn't true. For example, encourage others and try to bring them up when I'm with them. Once I do that, it isn't done, the same way something like climbing Kilimanjaro would be. No, goals like encouraging others are never 'done'. You do them, and then you need to do them again. These goals are not event-driven or one-off. They are not output-based. They are process-based. They go on and on, never complete, and your accomplishment of them defines who you are so much more than the accomplishment of any one-off goal you can have.

They are not conspicuous. Rowing the Atlantic Ocean is a phenomenal achievement and says a lot about how tough someone is. That is a spectacular goal. Encouraging someone who needs a push and making them feel better about themselves, quietly, every day? That is not spectacular. It's not phenomenal, nor is it conspicuous. But if I can do that and achieve that as a process-based goal, it will say so much more about who I am and will define me so much more than rowing the Atlantic or any other one-off achievement.

That is the space to which I am transitioning my goals – towards being processed-based. It is making me happier, more fulfilled, more consistently challenged to grow into the person I want to be, and is giving me many more opportunities to go to bed proud of myself. Isn't that what goals are for? I think you should try it. What are 3 process-based goals you could adapt in the next month that, if met, would make you a better person in the lives of those around you, and make you more proud of yourself?

One thing I'm planning for this Christmas is secret letters. Secret, unsigned, handwritten letters to people in my life who need a lift. They'll read it, they won't know who it's from, but they'll know that someone who knows them well thinks that they're amazing. How cool would that be?!

Step 1 Strategy

Step 1 Strategy is super simple and will make a big difference to you if you adapt it. It's front of mind for me every single day.

Most people have dreams and goals. They say things like 'I'd love to try this sport, go on this trip, start this business, learn this language' etc.. There are countless things we'd each love to do, try, experience and achieve. We're all very used to hearing about what the people around us want to do, and talking about our own dreams. What we're less used to, is hearing about people actually fucking doing them!

And I don't blame people for not doing the things on their bucket lists. It can be daunting and scary to embark on a journey, be it a trip, a business or learning a language. But the Step 1 Strategy exempts you from. The Step 1 Strategy only challenges you to take the first step. No long journeys or big challenges in sight, just do the very first thing you need to do. That will give you momentum. It will put you in the game, and you will be rolling after that.

The first time I really stuck to this was during my time in Google in Sydney. I had just MC's the National Conference and done a talk on my own story at it, and I got some really positive feedback. A lot of people came up and told me that I should do this professionally. That was on a Thursday.
That Saturday, I cleared my schedule. I spent the morning on Wix, putting a really simple site together, and the afternoon building an Adwords account for the site. Within a week, I had my first event booked, and all of a sudden, I had an events business.

That is Step 1 Strategy to a T. When someone tells you they set up and events business, it sounds impressive and multi-layered. It's not. Build a site, build an Adwords profile, and you're in business.

Pick a goal that you have in mind. What is the step 1 of that? What can you do that will put the ball in someone else's court. It could be something like emailing someone for a meeting so you can learn more about it. Whatever it is, do it. They'll respond, and all of a sudden you'll have momentum towards your goal.

Relationships

If you're a girl and you haven't had a boyfriend yet and that concerns you, please don't let it. What you have to realise is that these things happen at the right time for people, you need to just trust that. You also need to be aware that it could be the case that what you have to offer better than anyone else – your biggest competitive advantage in the game of love - might be something that guys your age just don't appreciate yet. Guys take a long time to wake up to the fact that the traits sought in a college girlfriend can be very different to the traits sought in a life partner. Please don't let this affect your confidence or your self-perception. Everything has its time.

The best thing you can do – and I think the thing that both sexes find most attractive and value most as they mature – is to just build a really good relationship with yourself. Keep evolving into someone that you really enjoy being and that you are proud to be, and trust me, the right guy will come along. I don't know why I'm singling out girls here, because the same message applies to guys. I guess girls are more expressive about this kind of thing, but guys do feel it too. We're all too young to worry about our love lives! Get out and about, enjoy yourself, build a great relationship with yourself, and I guarantee you that the right person will see that, and will want a relationship with you too.

People fall in love with people who have a *healthy* love for themselves. An unhealthy love for yourself is usually characterized by vanity or ego. A healthy love for yourself is usually characterized by a happy outlook, an enjoyment of the life you are living, and an ability to be genuinely happy for the success of those around you. Go get that, and you will attract the right people.
Build it, and they will come.

Part 3 – Career

I remember 2 years ago when I just had no idea what I wanted to do with myself, I was telling my mom how worried I was about my career and my future. I remember her saying something like 'But Mark you're so driven', as I always had been. It was in that moment that I realised that, at that time, I in fact was not at all driven. It was in that moment that I realised that 'having drive' and 'being driven' are two very different things. Different because of one extra ingredient: Direction. Driven = Drive + Direction

Without direction, you can't be driven because, while you may have an engine, you aren't going anywhere.

Without direction, I was just full of latent drive, and so too are so many people out there our age. I guess what I'm looking for this part of the book to achieve is to get you asking yourself questions that might help you find, change or redefine your direction and what is driving you. To be driven is a great thing, but it is also a privilege. I think deep down, we all want to be driven. Driven people are happy. They're using their time on Earth, and they're usually living life on their own terms. But getting to that point isn't easy. It involves asking very hard questions, experiencing lots of lows, lots of internal and external doubt, and, from my experience, a good spell of time spent being utterly lost in this world. Maybe – hopefully – it'll be easier for you, though I have to say that Death has been an excellent coach for me in this area in particular.

I learned an awful lot about myself in this area when I left my first job in Australia's largest and most prestigious investment bank, Macquarie. My values were at odds with those I was confronted with in the bank, and that caused huge internal conflict. My skills – my natural advantages – were not being used at all, and I was 'playing to my weaknesses'. I remember a mentor there told me, when I told him I was leaving, that it was a good decision. He said that if I didn't like it and wasn't naturally designed for it, that no matter how hard I worked, eventually someone who loved it would come in and pass me out. They would love the work, so they'd spend far more time on it without any issue, while working long hours on something I hated doing would just cause friction in me. They'd be naturally inclined toward work of that nature, so every minute they spent doing it would be more efficient than mine. In the long run, I wasn't going to win. Self-awareness and good mentoring helped me realise that.

I hope that in the coming pages, you have a similar awakening before it costs you anything…

Intro to Career

Let's start by making one thing clear: there is no right or wrong way to look at career. The only way you can look at career the wrong way is if you look at it using someone else's eyes rather than your own. You must look at it from your own values.

What does the notion of a career even mean to you? There's no right answer. It could be your path to money and power, your ticket around the world, or your means of paying the bills and feeding your family. None of these is better than the other, so firstly, chill out. Many of the people who had the most successful careers ask the same existential questions that you do.

Matter of fact, what career means to you might well change over time. It might be your road to riches now, but then you'll realise that life is more multi-dimensional than you'd realised, and you'll scale back your career. It could be a means of travelling now, but then you shack up, have kids and all of a sudden have food and school fees to fork out for, at which point money becomes your main priority. It could be community and friends that you're looking for a job to give you now, and then in a while you might get sick of going out and just want to spend time with your family.

It'll change, probably a few times, and that's fine. All you can do now is ask:

'What does career mean to me now, and what do I want from it?'

'How can I see that changing in the next five years?'

'What are the downsides or dangers of me viewing it this way, and can I live with them?'

'Can I protect myself against these downsides in the event that my priorities do change?'

Here's a great story to get you thinking about careers in different terms...

The Happy Fisherman

There was once a fisherman in Brazil called Lucas. Lucas was a very happy, relaxed and content man, who had everything he wanted. He loved fishing and made a living from it. He loved his family, and got to spend time with them. He loved his friends and his community, and he played an active part in their lives.

One morning he was coming home from a successful fishing venture, during which he had caught enough fish for himself, his family, and a little bit to sell to the local store. This happened a few times a week, while on other days he only had enough for the family.

When he arrived at the shore, he was approached by a man in a suit, who introduced himself as Juan.

"That's a successful fishing venture you've had there, bravo!", Juan said to him. "If you're doing so well, why did you stop? Are you ok?"

Lucas replied with a smile on his face- the smile of a man that has all he wants: "Oh everything is fine, thank you. I always knock off when I have caught enough for myself, my family, and my friends. I try to get home in time to have lunch with my wife and kids. Then, we spend time together, I help the kids with their homework, and then we meet our friends and the community for dinner and some singing and dancing. I'm a lucky man!"

"Ah, my friend", said Juan, shaking his head and smiling. "You are missing such an opportunity! What you should be doing is going back out there and catching as many fish as you possibly can, then come in when you can't fish for one more minute. *Then* you go home and spend time with your family"

Lucas humoured him.. "Ok, and then what? There's only so much fish my family and my community need. Any excess will go to waste. And besides, I can only fit so much in my little old boat!"

"Well that is where I can help you. In a few months you will not just have one boat, but many!"

"May boats eh? Then what?"

"Well then you can bring in hundreds of fish in a morning!"

"Ok..and then what?"

"Then you can distribute them among all the towns in the area, and soon you will have a fishing empire!"

Lucas feigned excitement. "Wow! A whole empire! What next??"

Juan couldn't believe that Lucas couldn't see his vision. "Then what?? Then you can do whatever you want! You won't have to fish long hours every day. You can just fish for a hobby. You can go home at lunch time if you want, and just spend time with your family. Hell, you won't have to fish at all! In the evenings, you can have dinner with your friends instead of having to spend it out on the water! You don't understand how successful you could be!"

Lucas laughed. He put his arm on Juan's shoulder. "My friend, I'm afraid it is you who doesn't understand. You see, that is what I already do! I measure my success not on the size of the business I have, but the moments of joy that I have in my day. I am already more successful than I ever dreamed of being. I like fishing, so I don't want to stop doing it no matter how wealthy I become. I appreciate you approaching me, though. You are more than welcome to join my family for lunch, and you can see what I mean. Let's also get you out of that suit into something more comfortable, you poor thing"

The moral? Pretty straight forward. Most people see their career as a lot of time doing things you don't like but that pay you well, so that you can retire early on the excess money you have made. Basically, live an imbalance both ways. Overextend on the work first, so that later on you can overextend on the relaxation and fun. It's logical. It makes sense, and its not wrong. But neither is the outlook of the fisherman. Rather than achieving balance through staggered imbalance, Lucas achieved balance in everyday life; big picture and little picture. The generation before us might call that a 'Millennial Midset', or seeking instant gratification, and maybe it is. But that doesn't make it wrong. In fact, the reality is that we know more about happiness and balance than that generation ever has or ever will, simply there has been considerably more research done on it than there had been when those guys were growing up.

It's just up to you to decide what works for you.

Living from the Inside Out

This lesson is at the very centre of my relationship with Death. In its purest sense, it is perhaps too idealistic to be practical, but I strongly encourage you to take it onboard and try to apply it to at least one area of life – the more significant the area, the better.

All kids have dreams. They have dreams of being astronauts, firefighters, CEO's, adventurers, dancers, singers, athletes. Then, when they enter their teens, most of them realise that the chances of these dreams coming true are rather slim, and so they give up and join the herd.
Some, though, persevere. They keep pushing for their goals right through their teenage years and remain on track.
Then they hit college. They start drinking, they get confronted with the real world in small doses, and many fall off and join the herd then.
But a few remain, they stay optimistic right throughout college and keep shooting for their stars.
But then they graduate. Reality hits them over the head and they, too, give up and join the herd.
Very few actually continue to push forward and keep striving for their 'Plan A'.

Why does everyone join the herd? Partially because they weren't good enough, or they genuinely lost interest. Often because they were daunted by the amount of work required to achieve their goal. But by far the most common reason for people joining the herd is that the people around them – those who really care for them – told them enough times that joining the herd was the wisest, safest and most sensible thing to do.

What we forget in all of this is that these people, the ones giving the advice, are part of the herd themselves. They've shaped their lives this way, and every time they present the argument to you as to why you should do the same, it reinforces for them that they've made the right decision in settling for their Plan B. But that doesn't mean it's the right decision for you.

What does 'joining the herd' mean? It means looking out at the world and seeing how you can survive in it. Looking out and saying 'where can I fit in without getting in anyone's way and without getting trampled on?'. It means, in that sense, living from the outside in. Allowing the world around you to dictate who you are and what you do.

Living from the inside out is the exact opposite of this. Living from the inside out means looking inside yourself and saying 'what do I have to offer the world that nobody else can offer it?'. 'What colour can I paint onto society's canvas that nobody else can paint?', because every single person has their own unique colour to offer, and I can't but imagine what a beautiful world we would live in if everybody had the confidence to share their unique colour.

Living from the inside out is the most rewarding way a human can live. It is the only way to live if you are serious about absolutely satisfying your spirit during your time on Earth. It is the output of a thorough search, and is a reward that is the preserve of those who search thoroughly inside themselves to explore what exactly their colour is and how best to share it. You can't skip or short cut The Search, although there are a couple of exercises that can be done to get it started:

Exercise : The Venn Diagram

Simple.

Step 1: List the 3 things you're relatively best at. If you get 90% in French classes, you're really good a French. But if everyone else gets 100%, then you're relatively bad at it. Our relative strengths and weaknesses are our most relevant because its is relative to the world around us that our professional value is gauged. A good hint for this is to think about your natural skills. What are you just naturally comfortable or competent at that most people struggle with? For me, it was public speaking. For others people, it can maths, languages, storytelling, quickly grasping new concepts...the list goes on.

Step 2: For each skill listed above, write a list of careers/jobs for which that skill is a valuable asset.

Step 3: Find the job that is on all 3 lists. But don't just rush to find any job that can stretch across the 3. Be patient about it. Flesh it out. Write out the most niche skills for each that you know won't be applicable to the other 2, that'll get the brain thinking in the right way and will open your mind. Revisit it, and see what jobs keep popping up.

Step 4: To put an extra filter on this, look at jobs that serve a mission you believe in. Nothing will motivate or demotivate you more than the mission of the group you are working with and working for. In general, I try to work on things that I want to see get done. Sometimes I need to make compromises here and there, but it is a great thing to hold as a general rule.

The Ghandi Solution

Legendary human rights activist Mahatma Ghandi is known for many things. One of which is his oft-referenced quote 'be the change you wish to see in the world'. Great line, and great place to get started on your search. I strongly believe that a very important question that young people need to ask themselves is this: 'What change do I wish to see in *my* world?' Sure, solving world hunger or achieving world peace would be great, but it would be hard to motivate yourself to go and set about achieving those changes. Instead, look around the world that you occupy every day and see what issues you can play a role in solving. Think global, act local. If everybody acts locally, global action is taken.

What are you sculpted for?

Not physically, and not even mentally. I mean experientially. What has your life experience designed you for? Ever heard the saying 'to know where you're going, you need to know where you've been'? This is that saying, in action.

What have you been through, what has your environment skewed you towards, that predisposes you to excelling at /understanding a particular challenge / industry / area? Were your parents doctors? Were you inspired by a teacher? Was a family member or neighbour an entrepreneur? Were you great at art or music in school? DO you know someone with a struggle that is now close to your heart, and you could be motivated to solve that problem at scale?

Think about these things. You might find that there is a path out there that you are already – unknowingly – accelerating down – and perfectly designed for -just because of your past and present environments. Try to remember that we are sculpted more by our environment than anything else.

"This is it for me"

People our age today have this obsession with 'finding their thing' or 'finding their purpose'. It seems that what we want to be able to say about our careers or our love lives is something like 'this is it for me', as if to say 'the search is over'.

Why do I know this? Because nobody has been as guilty of this as I have been. Both with jobs and careers and relationships, I have, on many occasions, said to others and, countless more times, myself that 'this is it for me'. In fact, I've really tried to sell myself on it, seducing myself with the logic that, if I could make that true and allow that relationship or that job to really *be* it for me, then the search would be over. That I could finally stop asking existential questions and start living life with a quiet mind and a clear direction and purpose.

Not healthy.
Not even realistic.
Or at the very least, not probable.

How many people do you know who have truly 'found their calling'? Very few, I would guess. It's not a normal thing. I would say that its much less common than finding mutual love.

This goes back to the idea of the two levels that we live on – the societal and the human. They're connected, but they are not the same. Our generation has stopped realising that we are human beings operating in a society, not societal beings. That is to say, the experience we have of life on earth is a human experience, not a societal one. The feelings and the emotions we feel are human emotions, not societal emotions. Societal emotions don't exist!

The concept of finding your calling, as we describe it, is arguably more of a societal ambition than a human ambition. Doctors, lawyers, teachers and firemen etc – they are the lucky ones who have managed to feed their human ambitions – treating, defending, educating and rescuing – through societal roles that clearly fit their desires. But most of us don't have those ambitions. And worse still, some of us don't know what our ambitions even are!

So what can we do?

A few things:

Stop planning for the long term

Rarely is something worthwhile accomplished by accident.
We need some sort of a plan or a mission.
But how can we plan effectively in such an unpredictable life?

Well, first stop planning for the long term and start planning for the medium term. If there's anything Death has taught me, it's that the long term is not guaranteed. With Sudden Death Syndrome, I worried for the first few years if I would even reach the age of 30. As far as I was concerned, I had no long term, I only had a short term. So what did I do? I lived around that short term and didn't worry about long term consequences. I went out 4 nights a week for 2 years and, most of those nights, would drink between 10-13 pints of Guinness. After 2 years of this, I went in for a heart check up and was told I was walking around with a pumping function that was just above the level of heart failure. The doc asked me why I was drinking so much and I explained my outlook. He told me that I definitely had no long-term future if I kept going the way I was going, so I stopped. I quit drinking, I lost 10kg of body fat, I got super fit and I started planning for the long term.

Over the past 5 years then, my heart has played up four more times, bringing me face to face with Death on several other occasions. Twice while I was working in the bank, once when I was working in Google, and once, years before, when I was holidaying in Fiji. The Fiji event taught me nothing.
The first episode while in the bank taught me that I needed to stop thinking long term and start living a life I actually enjoyed now. The long term wasn't guaranteed.
The second episode in the bank taught me that, 9 months after the first episode, I still hadn't made the change I said I would. It taught me how hard it was to make that change, and to shift from long term planning to short/medium term planning. But it also taught me that I had to make that shift. Two months later, I had left the bank. I can tell you this – quitting your first job is extremely nerve-wracking, but highly rewarding and growth-inducing. For me, it was the first big decision I had ever made totally in-house, and the experience of it taught me a lot. I recommend that young people try different jobs early in their career, for no other reason than the perspective that it lends to you on the working world and your role in it.

Back to the heart problems and meetings with Death.
The Google episode – the one last year that marked the beginning of the worst time of my life - taught me that my time in Google was up and that I needed to go and do the things I'd always wanted to – quit Google, write a book, start a business and travel South America. Within three months I'd done three of those, and the fourth came four months later.

What I'm saying is this. Long term planning is not always as good an idea as people give it credit for. You don't know who or what you'll be in the long term. You don't know what you'll want. You don't know what you'll value. You don't know what your circumstances will be, and you don't know if you'll even be alive or not. Why would you try to devote your life to someone who you know so little about? Do you really think you can guess that right, 40 years out?? With 40 years of life to live in between in a world that's changing as fast as ours is? I think that's crazy!

But I'm also not advocating living for the short term. That's what I did and it almost killed me. I see people do that now, just go travel aimlessly, and in many circumstances that's fine, but in many more it could be damaging. Living purely for the short term can be reckless and indulgent and can come at a medium- and long term cost.

So, what I advocate is living and planning for the medium term. Who- where – what - how - do you want to be in 5 years' time? Ten years, max, no more. Ten years is more long term in our world. I have a much better chance of understanding the guy I'll be in five years' time and serving his needs correctly now, than I do of serving the guy I'll be in ten years' time. I'm also likely to have much more in common me Me+5 than I will with Me+10, so doing what will please and serve Me+5 is also more likely to please and serve the person I am now. Then, when I'm him in 5 years, I'll have a better chance of serving the guy I'll be ten years from now, and so on.

Our generation has started to reject the 'planning for the long term' thing. That's for sure. Nothing too ground breaking here on that. My fear, though, is that those who have rejected long term planning have done so to too extreme an extent. They have bounced all the way over to just serving their short term, which is far from optimal either. The term YOLO, which still drives a lot of big decisions for people, could easily be described as an entire generation's off-the-shelf excuse for indulgent and irrational behaviour.
Serving the medium term protects your long term and also your short term, and is the very clear optimal strategy for us going forward. You can work hard without sacrificing all of your 'fun twenties', and you can travel without being anxious about what you'll do when the trip ends and you're faced with responsibility.

To summarise: Instead of seeking to be able to say 'This is it for me', instead, aim for 'this is what I'm enjoying right now, and I like the direction it's taking me in'. Enjoy both.

Discover Your Values & Strengths

"Your twenties are for learning and your thirties are for earning."

That's what my Macquarie mentor told me when I told him I wasn't going to join Google because of the $40k pay-cut. Before he told me the above, he told me I'd be a short-sighted idiot not to take the job.

Don't focus your income in your twenties. Don't get down if you earn below average, don't get complacent if you earn above average. The best jobs in your twenties are the ones that challenge you, educate you, and show you where you're strong and weak.

"Your twenties are for learning"

That 'learning' refers to learning skills, learning about markets, learning about how people work within your area etc. Of course. But above all – by far the most important area of learning to which this line refers – is learning about yourself.

Where are you strong? Where are you weak? What excites you? What bores you? What type of challenge do you enjoy? How do you respond to adversity? How relentless are you? What are your priorities in work? What are your priorities in life? What are your values? What are the challenges or problems that you want to see solved and want to work on?

So many questions! In the context of career and, to some extent, in the broader context of life, the above are the most important questions you can ever ask yourself. They are course defining. And there isn't a right answer to any of them. In fact, not one answer to any of these questions is better than any other answer. Seriously, not one.

Here's why. Nature – which incorporates human life – is not linear and not defined the way we like to define right or wrong, better or worse etc. Take for example, the question 'how relentless are you?'. We'd all like to think of ourselves as super-relentless, right? That shows strength. Relentless people are unstoppable. They're successful etc. But do you ever think about what goes hand in hand with relentlessness? Imbalance.

If someone is relentless at work, say Elon Musk, for example, that means they will work 100+ hours a week. They will take inordinate risk. They will place outsized priority on the task which they relentlessly pursue, and place undersized priority on every other element of life – family, friends, health etc. Now as an ambitious young guy, I always thought, when I heard something like this, that I would be the exception, but I'm not, and the chances are you won't be either. Something will suffer. You only have so much priority/energy/attention to give, and an overinvestment in A means an underinvestment in B. You could be ok with that. That's fine. You could be totally not ok with that. That's fine too.

There is no right or wrong to any of those questions, all that matters is that you ask them.

Discovering your strengths is equally important. Imagine an athlete who can sprint the 100m in 9 seconds being put in the shot putt team instead. He wasn't designed to throw shot putt, so he would be average. He would never win and he would be labelled an average athlete. In a parallel life, had he just tried out for the sprint team, he could have gone on to be an Athletics icon.

Who is responsible for his mistrialling?

Well, a few people. And that's where the working world is different. Because in the working world, nobody is responsible for the discovery of your talent except for you. In fact, the people you work with and for are likely to have a vested interest in you *not* shining, because your progress threatens theirs. This is particularly true in a big company, not a small one. That's the bad news: you're on your own.
The good news is that you have your whole twenties to figure it out. Everybody knows and accepts that becoming truly excellent at something is a very hard thing to do. What they haven't yet realised is that so too is finding the thing *at which* you can become truly excellent. That's where the real skill is. Many people stop that search before it is complete, and never realise their true potential.

I nearly did this in the investment bank. 12-14 hours a day on a spreadsheet is the exact opposite of what I am designed for, and I was going to stick it out for two reasons:

A) The money
B) I bought into some bullshit ideal about working on your weaknesses so that you could round out your skillset

'Round out your skillset'?? Are you kidding? We live in a world dominated by specialists. From finance to medicine to education to sport – everyone has a field in which they specialise. Why would I want to round out my skillset and focus purely on what I'm terrible at? That's nonsense. I did it and it nearly destroyed my confidence. Well, it did destroy my confidence, and luckily Google helped me to get it back. When I was in the bank I thought I had no future in business because I wasn't fast enough on a spreadsheet. Crazy. That work could not have been further from my natural work – the work for which I have been designed. Protect your confidence. Do your natural work that you're good at and you will shine.

Twenties for learning, thirties for earning: Learn what you're good at and what matters to you, then go and apply them and let them earn you money.
You'll find more success doing something you're good at - and doing it for a reason you buy into - than under any other circumstances.

There's a great story that highlights this theory. It's about two lumberjacks who were in a tree-chopping competition. Whoever could chop their tree down the fastest, won. When the starting whistle blew, the first guy did the obvious thing; he let out a big roar and just started swinging wildly into his tree; unrelentingly and with incredible force. Meanwhile, contestant number two put down his axe, walked up the tree and started examining it. He took ten minutes inspecting the tree, figuring out exactly where he would swing for and what direction he would come from. He then walked back down towards his axe. At this stage, the crowd around started murmuring – everyone talking about how much time this guy had to make up on contestant number one, who all that time had still been swinging like crazy.

Unfazed and seemingly unaware of his rival's progress, contestant number two caused further confusion among the crowd when he took his axe, sat on the ground and calmly began to sharpen it. Again, the murmuring picked up and the crowd were totally bewildered by this guy's bizarre behavior. Had he placed a large bet against himself??
Another five minutes passed and, still apparently oblivious to the presence of the crowd and his rival – who was fifty swings ahead at this point - contestant number two stood up and walked, with his sharpened axe, up to his tree. He perfected his stance in order to swing into the exact point that he had chosen to start on, and from the exactly perfect angle, he took his first swing. With his rival half way through his tree and starting to tire, contestant two remained completely calm and focused. He took his second swing into the same exact spot, then his third, fourth, fifth, hitting it in the exact same place every single time, consistently. After just thirteen swings in this precise manner, the tree started to crack and sway, and the fourteenth brought it down. The crowd were aghast, not least because the victor hadn't yet broken a sweat, but because it took so few swings to bring down a tree of such stature.

Many of us start our careers like contestant number 1. Exerting energy in every which direction, showing everyone how enthusiastic we are, and hoping that all of this exertion will pay off. This is wasted energy. Instead, we should be taking the time required to:

 - Look into ourselves.

- Look out unto the world.
- Find the exact pin point spot that we will look to make a mark on.
- Sharpen our axe – our minds and our skillsets – for that particular job
- Start swinging steadily and purposefully.

Humans vs Society & The 1ˢᵗ World Challenge

We are human beings – beings of nature – living and working in a structure known as society. We work in companies, we are subject to economic prevails, and we ourselves, as workers in this society, are economic instruments too.

But you already knew that. In fact, if you're anything like the average young professional today, that last sentence probably plays a strong role in forming your self-perception. And that, I have only recently realised, makes it - structurally - very, very difficult to achieve the fulfillment we are all seeking. Here's why:

We are human beings living in a society. We are not 'societal beings'. What is the difference? The source that we come from. Our fundamental make up. The laws we obey – biological and psychological rather than economic. We are derived of nature, not of economics or logic. We are from one world, while spreadsheets, dollars, economic inputs and economic outputs are from another.
Yes, we are social animals and so our role and our status in our society is a factor in our happiness and self-worth, but it is just one of several factors. If you limit your focus to just a fraction of the inputs, how do you expect to fulfil the rest? Focus in this case does not refer to time and headspace, it refers to self-worth. When you evaluate your self-worth, how do you weight the things that matter?

Health | Expression | Friendships | Family Relationships | Partner Relationship (if that's important to you) | Professional / Societal Progress | Human Contribution

With this in mind, let's take the example of Jonny. Jonny is 30. He is unemployed, overweight and has never had a girlfriend. In our society, with our skewed view towards economic value, Jonny is probably not scoring great. What you don't know, though, is that Jonny has some great, real friends who love him and value him hugely. He has a family that does the same. He volunteers at soup kitchens once a week, and on the weekends he loves to paint and is the happiest guy on the planet while he's doing so.

We went from looking at Jonny as a failure to a pretty cool guy who, yeah, is struggling in a few areas - he's human – but is really valuable to a lot of people. If Jonny died, it would be one less welfare cheque the state would have to write, but a family would have lost a loved one, many friends would be distraught, the lonely people at the soup kitchen would have one less friendly face to welcome them every week, and the world would lose a very happy artist. Jonny's life is seriously valuable!

Take a moment to look at yourself through the same lens now. You'll realise that you're a whole lot more valuable to the world than your CV or Linkedin profile might suggest.

Looking at this same theory then – humans vs society – in a more day-to-day lens, I think there are some important lessons to learn too, the biggest of which is that companies are not designed to make you happy. Even amazing companies like Google. They go to extraordinary lengths to make work a friendly and fun and fulfilling place for their employees - and they do a great job of accomplishing that – but at the end of the day, if the company fell on really hard times, a lot of those employees would be fired. They'd have to be, in order for the company to survive. I'm not saying it would be easy for management – they'd feel terrible doing it – but they'd do it, because just like any other company, Google's employees are its economic instruments.

The lesson?

We should never rely on work to fill our human needs.

We should never be surprised when company politics / happenings upset us. They're acting under a different set of laws to the ones under which we act, and which govern our emotions. When those laws conflict, we are exposed.

On the flip side, then, purely human behaviour is not likely to win out in company politics in the long run. Good Lord I wish it would, and I'm not saying it *never* will; I'm just saying that the odds are stacked against it, because again, the laws that dictate economic prowess are different to - and sometimes in direct conflict with – the laws that dictate human prowess.

'So what, I have to be a dick to do well at work??'

No. If you do that you'll get fired or kept down for being a dick. Just use your head rather than your heart when at work. Your heart deals with human stuff and your brain deals with logical stuff. Work is mostly logical.

No matter how advanced we may consider ourselves to be, we are all still subject to the human condition. That is what defines our existence and our journey through life. Something very important to note, is that the human condition has not changed. It has and always will be the same. What that should tell you is that, *whatever it is that you're looking for in this life, it is not to be found in anything outside of that which was accessible at the beginning of humanity. That is to say, it is not to be found outside of your Self, your interactions with other humans, and your interactions with nature. The human condition is impervious to materialism, to wealth, status or anything else we have since made up.*

In fact, materialism and all of the other things we have made up are what distract us from achieving happiness. Have you ever met someone who has done charity work or been to a really poor country? They always talk about how much happier the people are there compared to Westerners. Why do you think that is? I think it's because they're uncorrupted. They're missing the things we take for granted – education, food, water, safety – but they're also missing all of the bullshit distractions that constantly pull us away from happiness. They are living the real thing. They have the primal struggles that keep them stimulated the way natural beings like us were designed to be. They acknowledge and engage with each other, because they have no technology or anything else to dilute their attention. Their spirits appear free because they're not caged in materialism and consumption like we are.

Of course, our safety, water, luxury etc are nice to have for us. They are an advantage, and I'm not advocating giving them up. I'm pointing out that they are an advantage that come with a cost. That cost is that they provide us with an extra challenge that other people don't have. It's really hard for people to remain stimulated when they have access to literally anything in the world, be it food, clothes or sex, at the click of a button. It's really hard to enjoy material things without getting sucked into the vacuum that is materialism. They don't have these challenges in the third world. They have challenges that threaten their survival. We have challenges that threaten our happiness, and we – on an individual level – need to take those challenges seriously.

We tend to joke about First World Problems? This is *the* First World Problem, and it's a big one.

The Race

Around this time last year, I didn't like my job, I didn't know what I wanted to do, and all I knew was that I was going to quit and go travel South America. Now that I've done that, I've found things that I love doing, and I couldn't be happier.

One of my best friends right now doesn't like his job. He doesn't have a clue what he wants to do, and all he knows is that he is going to quit and go travel South America.

I'm a year ahead of him right?

Wrong.

This is a lesson that I, being a competitive person by nature, have taken a long time to get my head around. It's also a big one. The Ultimate, in a way.

I say the Ultimate because I have always been extremely sporty. Rugby, tennis, golf...any sport really. And I know how the scoreboard works in those sports. Get to 6 in tennis. Score more tries than the other team in rugby. Golf...let's not even get into how that bloody game works.
 But they make sense, and most importantly, you know who is winning and losing at the end of the game and right throughout.

That was what always frustrated me the most about life. Who was winning and losing?? Easy, the guy with more money.
Sure, that's what I thought, but that guy often has poor relationships, health or whatever else he has sacrificed to make that money – often times his own relationship with himself.
So it's not the guy with the money.
Fine. The guy with the family.
Maybe, but that guy struggles to pay his bills and seems to fight with his wife a lot. He also has bad health because he always drinks with his friends.

Ok, so not that guy...but now we're back to money...

And round and round we go.

I always go back to the meeting with Death on the gym floor last year with this, or to the hospital in New Zealand. When I was in both of those situations, I was right at the door on my way out of life. I was at the exit interview, where we all want to look at the scoreboard and see how we did. But there is no scoreboard. There are no points. I can actually tell you that. The first time, I didn't want to die just because I was too curious about what the future would have held for me had I kept living. But by the time the gym floor came around, which was my fifth interaction with Death, I had really learned a lot about how interesting and fun this life can be. I wasn't sad in an 'oh, but I'll never find out what the future held for me' way; I was sad in a 'wait, I'm just starting to realise how good this party is' kind of way!

That's the closest thing to a scoreboard that there is – and that looks nothing like a scoreboard! It looks nothing like a scoreboard because there is no universal score. There are no numbers. It's completely down to the individual. You could have a grumpy old man living on a hill who never socialises with anyone who, on the inside, is having an absolute blast! Seriously, he may get as much kicks out of complaining about the morning papers as you do from going on a night out or riding a rollercoaster. That sounds insane, but I'm telling you it's true.

The closest 'sport' I can liken life to is wandering the countryside for a day. Some people spend time in the woods and hate it, then they find the sea and love it and just spend all their time there. Some people like both and are happy to jump between the two. Some people spend the day doing jumping jacks. Some people spend the day birdwatching, while others sit around drinking, trying to figure out what could possibly be fun about birdwatching. Some people wish for rain, while others wish it away.

Not one of these activities is better than another. In this sport, the only winners are the ones who land on something they like, and the only losers are the ones who stop wandering for fear of getting lost or for fear of *being judged for not liking the same things as the people they started the walk with happen to like.*

That's it. That's my summary of life as a sport, taught to me by Death.

Now tell me, am I ahead of my friend who is about to go travelling?

I think not.

If I'm in the wrong relationship and he's in no relationship, he's closer to being in the right one than I am. Same thing applies to jobs.

So whether you think you're ahead or you think you're behind, you're wrong, because 'ahead' and 'behind' don't exist in this game of life.

The Fear

Every single person who has ever lived (apart from those alive right now), Death has met. He has been in more hospital rooms, nursing homes and funerals that we can even imagine. He once told me what he sees in the hospital rooms of the people who were too afraid to live life, who were scared of the world:

He told me of how he sees them on the bed beside the window, staring at the bland ceiling, not listening to the feint sound of the radio in the background. He sees them turn their head to look out the window, upon all that the world had to offer. He sees them recognize that all of the 'dangers' of the outside world were, in fact, only perceived dangers. He sees them recognize that the world won't even realize they're dead, because they never had the courage to let the world know they were ever alive. He sees them turn their head back to face up at that same, bland ceiling, just like they had done their whole lives. Then he hears them whisper, so that nobody can hear but themselves, "If I only I could have another chance".

Then, he relives them of their pain.

They say hell is what happens when, at the end of your life, you meet the person that you could have been had you had more courage. If that's true, I'm going to do everything I can to never go there.

The 3 Zones

In each area of your life, you operate in one of 3 zones: The Comfort Zone, The Stretch Zone, or The Panic Zone.

These zones are best illustrated using the analogy of a marathon runner. A guy says he'll run a marathon in 9 months' time. 45km. He's not that fit to start with. Here is how he approaches the challenge from each zone:

Comfort Zone: "I can run 5k now. I'll run 5k every week for 9 months and I'll be fine."

Stretch Zone: "I can run 5k now, but I need to run 45 in 9 months. I'll add 5k to my run every month, and gradually make my way there by pushing myself incrementally."

Panic Zone: "A marathon? Oh shit! I'm going out to run 45 km right now!" (He either gives up or has a heart attack on Day 1.)

We've all operated in all 3 of these zones. Needless to say, the Stretch Zone is optimal. The Comfort Zone guarantees 0% growth. The Panic Zone is characterized by heroic intentions and unsustainable undertakings, and the Stretch Zone is defined by compounded, consistent, incremental growth. That's where you want to be. That's where you're living on the edge:

Living on the edge of your mind – expanding it with new people who are into new things; Living on the edge of your physical capabilities – pushing yourself to be better/fitter/faster/stronger; Living on the edge of your professional capabilities – forcing yourself to grow. Living on the edge does not mean living dangerously. It means living for growth rather than comfort.

The most common and effective application of a comfort zone / stretch zone swap out is in relation to routines and regimens. We have all uttered the words 'I'm going to train every day for a month', or 'I'm going to start getting up at 6am on weekdays'. We've likely stuck to these intentions for a week or two, then given up and gone right back to our old ways. The key here is to go easier on yourself and just stretch – don't panic. Move your wake-up time from 8 to 7.30 for 3 weeks, then to 7, then to 6.30 and so on. None of these increments will shock you, you'll be able to consistently commit to them, and you'll reach you goal in no time, in a sustainable way. Gym routine, reading routine, same principle. Bite by bite, the elephant is eaten.

Expression

Express.
'Ex'- *Out*;
'Press'- *to push or squeeze.*

I don't think there's a secret to living a good life and being able to welcome Death with open arms next time he comes my way. But if I had to choose one thing, it would be expression, and that very word has become the very centre of my life and the thing that drives every single thing that I think and do.

Through my interactions with Death, my mission in life has become extremely simple:

'To identify every single thing inside of me that I can offer to the world, and *express* it out of me before I die'.

What's yours?

That's mine, and it takes many channels of expression for any of us to accomplish this, because as humans we are so multifaceted that, well, each one of us just has a whole lot to offer. For me, the main channels I focus on are:

- **Commercial Creativity** – I love business, I really do. I think it's a beautiful sport, just like tennis or rugby. You have great players who carry out amazing moves, and use those skills and moves to bring amazing products, services, organizations and cultural changes to the world. That, to me, is just amazing. It's blows my mind too much for me to even describe. The way most people have favourite athletes, I have favourite business people and favourite companies. My two are Nick Woodman and Yvon Chouinard, the founders, respectively, of my two favourite companies – GoPro and Patagonia. Google them. They're total mavericks.
- **Human interactions** – trying to use human interactions to brighten other people's day and, hopefully, walk away from an interaction with me feeling good about themselves. Again, 'The Great Man is the man who makes every man feel great'.
- **Books** – Projects like this where I try to articulate the lessons my unique experiences have taught me, in the hope that they might be of use to someone else. I have gained an incredible amount from reading about other people's experiences, theories and imaginative output, and I would love to be able to pass that on.
- **Poetry** – I love writing poetry and I know from my experience consuming it that it can be a great way to entertain/connect/inspire, and I'd love to be able to do that for others. If my 18 year old self heard that I wrote poetry, he'd beat the crap out of me, and the sad

part is, he could! But it just came out of nowhere and I love it now. I encourage you to explore random activities that take your interest and see where that exploration takes you.

- **Love & Relationships** – I have some single friends who, in a way, I wish weren't single because I know how much they have to offer someone else in a relationship. I want to make sure that if I'm in a relationship, that person gets the benefit of anything I have to offer. That's a very fulfilling channel for me.
- **Cause** – I think it's important for every human to have one cause that they're committed to serving, financially or otherwise, outside of themselves. It's proven to be great for happiness & fulfilment, and it of course would make a huge impact on the beneficiaries of that cause too. I really want to make a dent in the fight against childhood obesity. That passion too came out of nowhere, but now it's here and here to stay!

When I look at mental wellness – not clinical mental health but the wellness of everybody with no clinical or chemical mental health issues – I see expression as a core factor. I would venture to say that people usually find themselves in a state of poor mental wellness as a result of a lack of expression. People who don't feel they can express themselves in their relationship, in their work, in their own personal lives, to themselves, even…these appear to be common factors among people with poor mental wellness, and I worry that these cases go unflagged, unnoticed, and ignored until they evolve into poor mental health, which of course is a much more serious matter. People working long hours in corporate jobs, for example, rarely find a means through which they can freely express themselves, because they don't have time or energy and their jobs doesn't allow for it. This suppression persists for sixty-odd hours of the week, for thirty plus years. How do they *think* that's going to end?!

On the opposite end of the spectrum, those who enjoy the finest mental wellness often do so because they have searched for, found, and enjoyed different channels through which they can express themselves. They have found professions, partners, pals and past times that all allow the person to express themselves freely and in different ways. Not only does this let air out of the pressure valve that is the human mind, but it also provides the person with stimulation, enjoyment and a feeling of recognition that cannot be replicated by any other means.

As Henry David Thereau said: 'Most men lead lives of quiet desperation, and go to the grave with their song still in them'

That's my biggest fear, and that is what defines my relationship with Death.

Expression & Midlife Crises

I have always found midlife crises fascinating. How could someone who appeared so together just crack and go batshit all of a sudden? It never made much sense to me – how do they get themselves in that position in the first place?

But then I realised, that the term 'midlife crisis' is, itself, misleading. Misleading because, in your classic midlife crisis, what we call the crisis is actually just the effect of the crisis; the result of it. The *actual* crisis happened years before, when they didn't express or take in all that they now feel they need to express or take in. Going back to the 2 Acts brought up in Part 1, 'midlife crises' are usually triggered by a premature transition from Act 1 to Act 2. People go buy a sports car or join a rock band so that they can express things that they had trapped inside themselves and denied of an outlet for many years. I say get this stuff out early; ideally soon after it first hits you. Your priorities will change over time and you'll pick up innumerable responsibilities as you grow older. If you're young and free and you have something you're dying to achieve or experience, go and do it and do your future self a favour. Scratch your itches. I know for a fact that if I didn't go to South America last year, I would have some sort of crisis waiting in the wings for me. In fact, maybe last year was the crisis! Who knows, and who cares, because I did it. You should do whatever your version of that is, before you no longer can.

Your Tinder Strategy

When I do talks in companies, one of the things I talk the most about is Tinder. I tend to talk about Tinder for about 15 minutes, and I cover it all. I cover profile set up, who you match with, catfishing and falling in love.

Why.

I talk about Tinder because young people looking for hits on Tinder is just like young people looking for hits in the job market. They build their profile (CV), put their best foot forward, try to tell the other person what we think they want to hear, and try to have one or two things that make us look original, when in actual fact we all have the same 'originalities' on our profiles and CV's. Very similar markets. That's the profile.

Then we talk about catfishing. This is the really important part because employers get catfished more than just about anyone.
Employers have an amazing CV come through and they read all these amazing experiences – 'Tried a start-up in college', 'built houses in Kenya' and so on. Great grades. The employers get excited and they bring that person in for an interview. They think they've found their guy.

Guy shows up and everybody is all smiles. He sits down for his interview and they start asking questions.
"Tell us about your start-up in college"
'Sure. I was part of a team of 20 and we had this idea for 6 months and then study got too intense and we stopped'.
"Ok. What did you learn?"
'I learned teamwork entrepreneurship and leadership skills'.
Flat as a fucking pancake.
"Right. Great. And what about the house building in Kenya?"
'Great experience. Experience experience experience. African people are so happy'.

They say they'll be in touch. Next, in walks a girl. No start-up. No Kenya. Less impressive grades. They only gave her the interview because she kept hounding the HR team with emails.

Girl walks in. First question:
"What's with the grades? They're below our threshold. Usually we would let people in if they had amazing experiences to justify poor grades but in this case we don't see any…"
'Yes, I was looking after my granny for the past year. She's been really sick and it's been really hard for all of us. I've been trying to squeeze college in but it hasn't been easy. I've looked at your firm though and I like the direction it's going

in. I saw that you have the XX team, are there any grad role in that by any chance? Looks like fascinating work'.

Deliberate. This girl is a fucking grown up. Her profile wasn't great but when she showed up, it was clear that she had lived her own life, not one she felt would look good.

Here's the lesson. We can go around doing things to say we have done them, as many young people do either in order to build their CV or to keep up with peers; But if we do that and aren't actually engaged with the activity – if it's not something we're actually passionate or curious about – then that will come off when we're talking to employers. You're just sending the message that you haven't made the transition into an autonomous, independent-thinking adult yet. The employer looks at you and thinks,

    A) This person is a sheep (and if they hire a sheep, that says a lot about the job), and

    B) This person is a flight risk because if they haven't learned to think for themselves yet, they might do so half way through the contract and leave.

What we need to do in order to avoid this, is go and have own our experiences. Do the things we actually want to do, do things on our own so that we carry weight, not like that guy in the start-up of 20 people, each of whom did next to nothing. Carry weight. Be authentic, Be the real deal. Expose yourself to social risk and other threats to your comfort. Follow your imagination. Push your own boundaries. Yes, some employers will
swipe left and not hire you. The important thing is that the right ones will. You end up in a role that you're actually suited to and that you'll perform well in, and that is as good as it gets either in the employment market or on Tinder!

Hustle & Pride

What is a good life? I guess it's just a long string of good days, isn't it? So a better question is, what is a good day?
This is a question I've asked myself many times and have enjoyed trying to answer. So far, this is the best I've got:
The keys to a good day are hustle and pride.

No human was designed to sit down watching TV all day. Humans are designed to be up and about, hunting and gathering, growing, being challenged. Climbing, falling and climbing again. As the great (and insane) Hunter S Thompson wrote – one of my favorite quotes of all time:

"Life should not be a journey to the grave with the intention of arriving safely in a pretty and well preserved body, but rather to skid in broadside in a cloud of smoke, thoroughly used up, totally worn out, and loudly proclaiming "Wow! What a Ride!"

Life is boring when we're not doing anything, trying anything. Life is even boring when we *are* doing something but it's old and mundane. Life is about hustle.
Having a reason to get up in the morning and chase after something. That is what our ultimate ruler – Nature – designed us to do. If we resist that, we don't fulfil our purpose.
Speaking of purpose, there has actually been extensive research showing that having a reason to get up in the morning - a purpose in one's life – fuels better physical health, better relationships and a longer life.
Now, there is a balance. Stress is the silent killer that creeps in when you go too far. Boredom is the silent killer when you don't go far enough. And if you go just the right distance – if you hustle consistently and merrily, you win it all.

But then work is over and you have to go home. What then? More hustle? Not necessarily, you deserve a break. You have other elements of your life – hobbies, relationships etc – that need investing in.

What's next here is pride.

If you come home proud of the work that you have done during the day – proud of what you have contributed to society and proud of the quality of work that you have produced – then you can go home and put your feet up, fulfilled and happy, proud of your day's output.

Add in some laughter, some socializing, good food and some good lovin', and you have had one hell of a day. Get a run of them going, and you're in for a hell of a life!

How do you want to stand out?

I think it is fair to say that individualism is a key component of the make-up of a millennial's identity. Millennials don't want to be told 'you fit into this crowd of people, you are all the same'. They want to be told 'you are totally unique, you don't belong to any crowd, and you are amazing'.

We all want to stand out. At least, I know I certainly do. And this has been a struggle at times because, frankly, standing out is a competitive game – lots of people want to do it.
I think a big step I made in this area happened when I identified what area it was that I wanted to stand out in. Did I want to stand out for being extremely professional? Did I want to stand out for being exceptionally well-paid and hard working? Did I want to stand out for being exceptionally creative, or an exceptionally thoughtful human being? There are a million ways in which we can stand out from the crowd. I guess it helps to pick one and go for that first. Of course you can be exceptional in several fields, but choosing which one matters to you the most right now, might just serve as a reminder of why being exceptional matters to you in the first place. It might reinforce your reasons for wanting to be exceptional and ensure that those reasons are in line with your values.

Something I alluded to earlier in this book is the idea of being inconspicuously exceptional. That is, being exceptional without being the entrepreneur or the professional athlete or the exceptionally attractive one or whatever else. Try being exceptionally warm, exceptionally friendly, exceptionally well-read, exceptionally thoughtful, exceptionally positive...anything at all. There are literally thousands of avenues. Think of ways in which you would like to be considered exceptional. Think of why you would like to be exceptional and be considered exceptional in those ways, and then think of what you can do, starting with one act in the next 24 hours, to begin your journey towards being exceptional in that way.

Those who know how and why they want to be exceptional have a much better chance of actually achieving it.

The search for Identity

People talk about how teenage years are such a difficult and confusing time in a person's life. Personally, I didn't find this to be true, simply because I was interested in nothing other than sport and rugby, so that's the only thing that I paid attention to. For better or worse, I was as unconfused and as one-dimensional a teenager as you were ever going to meet!

Similarly, people talk about the transition into adulthood as a very difficult and confusing time. Sure, we are not subject to biological forces like puberty, working to change and challenge our physical and hormonal state/form, like we were during the teenage years, but we are subject to a plethora of psychological, emotional and societal forces that work to change and challenge our mental and emotional state and form.

At the core of this is the struggle for identity. The struggle for identity is part and parcel, not just of the human package, but of the package of any social being; we reach a point in our life when we morph into a weight-baring member of our community, and we struggle to identify what kind of weight-baring community or society member we wish to be.

Furthermore, it is true of millennials that we put extra pressure on this search for identity as it relates to career decisions, simply because we millennials allow our careers to define who we are more than any other generation has. That's part of our culture, and like it or not, nobody is immune to the culture that surrounds them. The extra pressure is what makes this harder, because where peoples' careers used to answer the question 'What are my skills?', today their careers play a major role in answering the question 'Who am I?'. This question being asked by the masses leads to mass confusion. Effectively, the questions being asked have changed. We used to ask two questions: 'Who am I?', and separately, 'What are my skills that I can build a career on?'. Now we ask 'Who am I, and what career reflects that?' We're putting two filters on the answers we're given, making the options much narrower and harder to find.

"Who is Mark Maxwell?"

This is a question I have asked myself thousands of times over the past 8 or 9 years. It's the biggest question one asks during their life, and it results in countless follow up questions:

What do people see when they look at me? What values are my name attached to? What do I represent to the people who know me? What have people come to expect from me, behaviour-wise, output-wise, principle-wise and so on?

All very real questions. I guess my interactions with Death have made me ask these questions with a little more intensity than perhaps most people would, but I consider myself very fortunate for that to be the case. Meaning well is one thing, but when it has no will behind it, it won't take you very far. Only with will do our thoughts become actions and those actions become our identity.

I guess what I have come to realise, or, dare I say 'conclude' on this matter, is that identity is a very, very fickle thing, whether that is who you are to the people around you, or who you are to yourself. I refer to the careers chapter when I said that all I am is a vessel. I am a vessel that is measured and evaluated on my output alone. If I am a bully for years, I will be known as a bully. People will ask what I'm like and they will be told that I'm a bully. From that moment on, the behaviour that that person will expect from me – the output of the vessel known as Mark Maxwell – will be the behaviour of a bully. My self-identity – who I am in my own eyes – might perfectly agree – I might think I am a bully.
But then, on a random day, I might commit a random act of extraordinary kindness, surprising even myself. All of a sudden, my identity, both in my eyes and in the eyes of all who are

aware I committed the act, changes a little, like a glass of water with some dye dropped in it. All of a sudden, I am (still) a bully, but now I am a bully with the capacity for extraordinary kindness. My identity – built up over years of bullying - is starting to transform after that isolated act. Add another drop of dye in (another act of kindness), and now it transforms more. The colour changes further. Before long, the glass of water - my identity – might be a totally different colour, and I go from being known as a bully to being known as an extraordinarily kind person. Identities are fickle things. They can dramatically change very quickly.

Identities are also very fluid things, and that is very important to recognise for young people. They are never constant. Whoever you were in school, whoever you are now, you will never be again. There is a great Eastern proverb, which states that the same man never walked into the same room twice, because both the man had changed and the room had changed each time. The man who walked in was different to the man who sat down, etc. We are constantly changing, and you get to control the direction and the intensity of that change.

Why is this useful to you? It's useful because it is a rare reminder to you that you don't decide upon an identity and then just run with it. You just face each decision, each moment and each interaction individually, and your identity will be made up of the manner in which you approached and navigated those interactions. Don't pressure yourself to decide upon an identity. Just maintain a mind that is open to novelty and change, and give everyone you come into contact with, either socially or professionally, the best experience of you that you possibly can.

I changed enormously during my time in Australia, to the point where, when I returned, my friends recognised me physically but barely recognised me personality-wise. Did I want to change? I don't think so. I think I was given the catalysts for change – on my own on the other side of the world, in an investment bank, then a huge change of environment into Google, first real girlfriend, all new friends, travel, heart issues etc. Most of my change came as a result of my environments changing. I could have resisted it, but what good would that have done? To change is to grow. Yes, you'll change away from old friends and towards new ones. You might even change out of a career path or a relationship, and towards new ones. That's scary, but you have to embrace it. To resist change is to resist growth, and to resist growth is to suppress your own potential.

How can you trigger change? Start with your environment. Go out and meet new people – not more people from your world, but people from a whole different walk of life. People who are wired differently to you and are driven by different things. Listen to them. Try to wrap your head around their outlook. Try to see the lines of logic that they see, which mightn't come naturally to you. I'm not saying you need to agree with their viewpoints, I'm just saying you need to open your mind to the point of being able to see them. That will foster change. Challenge yourself physically, professionally and creatively. That too will foster change.

Last point on this: changing does not mean 'not being yourself'. I talk about not being who you were in school or whatever and people think 'oh, he means going off and pretending to be someone else'. Not the case. I mean allowing the wind of life to take you in the direction you're meant to go in. Embrace that change and you can spend all of your energy moving with it in that direction and preparing to arrive at whatever your destination is. Resist that wind and you will waste a huge amount of your time and energy doing so – trying to remain who the people who matter in this chapter of your life want you to be and remain to be. Or worse, people from the last chapter. The person the people from your last chapter want you be was probably a teenager. Teenagers don't survive in the adult world.

I'm ten years out of school next year. The people I know who are happiest from my class are those who have embraced change. They are thriving. They have moved jobs, tried different things, grown and are thriving doing things that a lot of them thought they would never or could never be doing. The others – the ones who tried to live in the past, are only now waking up to the fact that that cannot be achieved, and they are only now starting to look at what way they are going to survive in this grown up world.

As Charles Darwin said, "It is not the strongest of the species that survives, nor the most intelligent. It is the one that is most adaptable to change".

"Ugh, I just don't feel like I have any, like, Purpose"

How many times a week do I have to hear this crap? Obvious response:
"Go work for a charity"
'No, because I still want money'
"Then keep your high paying job and do charity work on the side"
'Hah! Yeah, sure, and just, like, *not* watch Love Island?'

It's a real thing. People want to make money, they want to feel that they have a purpose, and they want to chill out and watch Love Island or whatever else they're into. They want to be fulfilled. Everyone does, and we all have the right to be fulfilled.

How and ever, we do not have the right to be fulfilled *easily.* Fulfilment is the one thing that every human on earth wants. Some people want to be rich, some people want to have a family and aren't concerned with money, some people just want to be happy, whatever that might mean for them practically; But everyone wants to be fulfilled.

Just like anything else of value, being fulfilled is not cheap. It's not easy. You have to work for it, possibly harder than you have to work for your money. The person who won't do charity work because it clashes with Love Island has as low a chance of being fulfilled as the person who won't get out of bed before lunchtime has of being rich. Not impossible, but the odds are stacked against them because they're not willing to be proactive in making it happen.

And that work – that input – isn't all manual, actual work. A lot of it is just searching. Searching for a problem to solve that you actually really want to see solved. I tried a few different charity things in Sydney and, while it was nice to do them, I didn't really get much out of it. It didn't give me what I was looking for and so I was less likely to keep it up over the long run. Then I started noticing how I reacted when I saw an obese child and I realised that I had struck on something. I started researching the problem, the anger in me grew and all of a sudden, I had a purpose. Three years after starting to look for one, I finally found a problem that I really, deeply wanted to solve.

Purpose is hard to find. Go and talk to people who have clearly found theirs. If you can't ready about the, Not for the sake of you being able to jump on their thing and hope that you become passionate about it too, but so that you can learn about the journey they took to find that passion. The ways of thinking that they used. You can then draw alignments to your own journey or use the same thinking models to arrive at a suitable pursuit for you. Besides, when you do meet these people who are just totally bought into a cause, it's incredibly refreshing and energising.

Can you think of anyone like that in your life?

The rule of 35

Here is a good rule of thumb for your careers. I have heard this, I didn't make it up.

In your career, no matter if you are a grad or have been at the company for 40 years, an effective mindset to have is to always act like you are 35.

Why? Why should a grad do this?

A grad should do this because it will prevent the grad from doing something that slows the majority of grads down – hiding from responsibility and not committing to the role. It will drive the grad to step up to the plate, try to look at problems with an owners' perspective and work with a more mature approach.

Why should someone older than 35 apply the rule of 35?
Someone older than 35 should apply the rule of 35 because 35-year-olds generally work the hardest. They are forward thinking, they are pushing for leadership roles, they have young families to provide for and mortgages to pay off. They have visions for where they want to take the business and they have the time and energy to make those visions happen. Doing this will enable a person who has been in the workforce for a long time to avoid the traps of laziness and looking backwards rather than forwards. They will still develop their own visions and be stimulated by the effort to make those visions come true.

Keep within the lines

The moral lines and the lines that outline your best interests.

Lots of people do bad things. Most hard drug users do lighter, social drugs before the hard stuff. They say – and I've seen this first hand – that they would never do anything more serious than weed or alcohol, and two years later they're spending half of their disposable income on cocaine. I've seen that, first hand. The line they said they'd never cross just moved closer, as soon as they crossed the first line.

Most hard-core criminals started out as petty criminals. They robbed the odd house or corner shop, and claimed they'd never sell drugs or kill people. A few years later, they did.
The line moved.

Jeff Skilling ran Enron and was a Rockstar Fortune 500 CEO. He then got 14 years in prison for turning Enron into the most corrupt and criminal company in US history. I have heard classmates of Skilling's from Harvard say that he was a good guy, but he crossed one little line and then another and then another, and next thing he knew he was destroyed and rotting in prison while his kids – the ones he was doing all that to provide for – grew up with a disgraced surname and no father.

The point is this: Everyone you have ever called an asshole (think of them now) probably didn't mean to be an asshole. Nobody wakes up in the morning and says 'I'm going to be an asshole today', or 'I'm going to kill as many people as I can in my life', or 'I'm going to graduate Harvard and become the biggest disgrace in the history of capitalism'. Nobody plans for these things. Neither did Jeff Skilling. Just like you and me, these people never even think that they'd be capable of the horrible things they do. But they cross one line and say it's a once off, then they cross another and they say 'that's it, I'm done crossing lines'. But those line crossings reinforce bad behaviour and change that person's outlook. They might even give them a thrill, and from that point on, that person is a line-crosser.

Do yourself and everyone in your life a favour. Don't cross lines. It's rarely worth it. As Clayton Christensen said, "It's easier to stick to your principles 100% of the time than 98% of the time". Your life is a string of extenuating circumstances, and every time you say 'just this once', you are crossing a line that will be very hard to come back from. Whether your vice is alcohol, drugs, cheating, chocolate or swearing, it's probably easier for you to cut that behaviour out entirely than to control it and limit it.

Essay Task

I know a university lecturer named Nacho (Ignacio). We have these really deep conversations, from which I take away a lot more than he does – he's the wisest and happiest man I've ever met. I once asked him, while I was really struggling with the PTSD last year, what he thought the meaning of life was. Here's what he said:

"Every term, when my new class comes in, I give them an assignment to do before the second class. I tell them to create for me a 'complete expression'. A book, a poem, an essay, a song; anything. It can be in any structure and it can be about anything. No title, no limitations, no restrictions whatsoever. And you know what the students do? They complain! They complain that I never gave them any direction! They complain that I gave them choice! They *complain* that I gave them freedom, and autonomy, instead of giving them boundaries and rules!"
"I feel that this assignment to my students is like life for all of us. We have been put here, with no direction, and told to create a complete expression. That's it. A complete expression, of any kind we choose. No limitations whatsoever. Now, some people skip the assignment altogether, while others get so unsettled by the absence of boundaries that they can't choose what to express and end up expressing nothing; instead choosing to spend their lives looking at what everyone else is doing and criticizing it or thinking of reasons why they can't choose a similar expression."

"Then, there is a small group who come back and give a complete version of whatever it is that they had inside of them. Some are brilliant, and some are mediocre. Never mind, I give everyone in this group the same mark: 95%. It is the effort and the level of expression that is important, not its quality."

"And lastly, there is the smallest group. Usually, this is even one person a term if I'm lucky. This person gets the best mark in the class. They come back with a work of art, with a sculpture or something else that is completely different to what the rest of the class did. And you know what?" he laughed, "It is usually terrible! But it gets 100% in my class, because I know that that person has searched for what he wanted to express and how he would express it. He explored the possibilities outside the confines of what I had suggested, and he disregarded the approach that everyone else was taking in order to create a unique expression."

"So you ask me, Mark, what life is about, and I tell you. Life is just another assignment to create an expression. The question is, can you make it unique, and can you make it as true a reflection of what is in the deepest depths of you as can possibly done? You are the only person in history and in future who can accurately express what is inside you. Doing that makes a remarkable life. Doing it well makes as fulfilling a life as can be lived."

Part 4 – Outside the Self

Time

Had I stayed dead that morning in Auckland in January 2011, two weeks before my 19th birthday, many things would have been said about me thereafter. Lots of good things, some bad things, and lots of exaggerated bullshit that's said at every funeral and has thus lost all meaning. But the one thing that would have been said more than anything else would have been along the lines of:

'He was so young, if only he'd had more time'.

Now that's fair because, sure enough, I was pretty young to die. But what about the other half of that statement: 'if only he'd had more time'. If only I'd had more time…what? What would that have given me? A chance to live one more ordinary life out there? Come back to Ireland, go to college, apply for a load of jobs I didn't want and take the one that looks like it sucked the least? Go through that for a few years, put on a load of weight because my job has drained any appetite for life I'd ever had, and then find a girl who will listen to me complain about my career as long as I'll listen to her bitch about hers? Find a TV show to numb the pain a few nights a week and spend the rest of the time talking about other peoples' Instagram accounts and complaining about their values, even though I am committed to spending 70 hours a week for 50 consecutive years trying to emulate it as closely as possible. Of course I would contribute my fair share to the destruction of the planet because I've been trained to give a fuck about nothing outside of promotions at work, and I'd always have alcohol or harder drugs there to numb the pain and make sure that I never ventured outside my weekly cycle, for fear of what I might find.

That sounds miserable, yet it is very closely aligned with the life lived by most modern professionals. It's horrible. It's a life lived by the body, but not by the soul. I mean, where does the soul get reached in any of that described above?

Death has taught me that time is our most valuable asset. Not money, not property, not love. Time. You can't make it, you can't earn it, and you don't know how much you get. With it you can do absolutely anything, and without it you can do absolutely nothing. How we spend it defines us as humans. If you want to know who someone is, look at who and what they invest their time in. If you want to know what someone's future looks like, look at who and what they invest their time in.

Money can be saved, shared, invested or spent. It can also be wasted.
Time, on the other hand, can only be invested, spent or wasted.
What is the difference?

Invested time is put into a person or activity with a view to getting value back for that time in the future.

Spent time is put into a person or activity with a view to getting value back immediately.

Wasted time is put into a person or activity when no value is returned – no entertainment, education, enjoyment, inspiration…nothing.

Needless to say, I think the majority of our time should be invested while we're young, and the rest spent. Wasting your most valuable resource when you have no idea how much of it you have left? That seems downright strange to me – especially living with Sudden Death Syndrome (SADS).

How would you live if you had SADS?

Where do you currently invest your time? Where do you spend it? What do these answers say about you?

Trips to The Temple

There is something that seems very obvious to me that, when I think about it, I cannot understand how it isn't a widely held view. That is the idea, or, perhaps, fact, that Nature is God.

God, for want of a better term, is the name that Christians and other people around the world have given to an Energy. Muslims call this energy Allah. Other groups have different names for it, but the energy – no matter what one calls it – is generally deemed to have some shared characteristics and responsibilities in our universe:

God created the world
God created us
God is the all-powerful force that we should revere and fear
God is love
God is what brings us all together as a race
God is awesome – ie: we react to God with awe
God is wonderful – we react to God with wonder

Now let's see if we can't sneak 'Nature' into these sentences without making sense of them:

Nature created the world: We live in a natural world, which operates under a system that we have named 'the laws of nature'.
Nature created us: We are natural beings who also fit and operate within the laws of nature. We feed off the planet's output. We are living, breathing mammals.
Nature is the all-powerful force that we should revere and fear: Remember tidal waves? Lightening bolts? Hurricane Caterina? Lava spills? Mudslides? Avalanches? Nature makes the rules. We're just ants trying not to get in the way.
Nature is love: Or more accurately, love is a natural thing. Again, we're natural beings. Love is a feeling that happens within us and between us, making it a natural thing too. We see it in how birds, animals and fish protect their tribes and offspring. Love isn't some mystical thing that we have to attribute to something going on in the heavens. It's an instinct from our natural world, shared by many living things, not just humans.
Nature is what brings us all together as a race: No man is an island. If he was one, he wouldn't last long. Loneliness is scientifically proven to be almost as bad for us as smoking. We need each other to survive. So too do penguins, and many other species. Laws of nature, people.
Nature is awesome and wonderful: Think sunrises, sunsets, waves, wildlife, Aurora Borealis, snow-capped mountains, starry nights, shooting stars, beautiful people, beautiful gestures that make our eyes well up….it's all nature. All of it.

Why do a disproportionate amount of priests rape kids? Because they have this vow of celibacy that they've signed up to, that is in direct conflict with the laws of nature to which they belong. Move in direct conflict to nature and, in the long run, you are likely to eventually have the urge to lash out in some way – your body is being forced to function against the laws by which it was created.

Why are climate change and extreme weather events becoming increasingly severe threats against humanity? Because we have operated in direct conflict with the laws of nature for a sustained period of time. That's God we're working against – what did we *think* was going to happen?

Why do we feel great when we feel a real connection with someone? A stranger, a lover, a friend or a family member. Because we are tribal beings. Introvert or extrovert, we thrive off interactions with our fellow man. That's a law of nature at play.

When I pray, I pray to nature. When I am praying and asking that something will happen, that something is invariably at the effect if nature in one way or another, and so it is nature that I need to conspire with me to make it happen. Nature is *it*. It is the beginning and ending of it all. I try to go to the temple once a week. Not a church, and not a synagogue. The outdoors. That is the real temple. Spend a day in the outdoors and you will come back feeling everything someone should feel after an interaction with the Ultimate Power.

Money

There's a contradiction among our generation that I find very interesting. We are a generation who vindicate the pursuit of material wealth – people are often ashamed about admitting that they want to be rich because the inevitable judgement that our generation will cast upon them – yet we spend an enormous amount of time talking about celebrity, tracking celebrities and 'ballers' on Instagram, and aspiring to the very things that money can buy. Why are we so open about wanting it and yet so judgemental of those who admit they are going after it?

Death has given me some great insights on this.

There's something you should know here as a preface. I know this. My friends and family know this. Death knows this and so should you:

You will never meet an 18-24 year-old as focussed on making money as I was. They just don't exist. I was obsessed with it. But why? I was never even a materialistic guy! I remember, in fact, a friend saying to me that if I were to get rich, it would be an enormous waste of money, because I wouldn't even use it. So why then? Did I want to get rich so I could give it all away to charity? That's certainly what I claimed was the reason, but that's bullshit too. Even back then I'd realised that it wasn't worth committing every ounce of myself to getting rich if I was going to give it all away, especially when, realistically, the person who could get rich instead of me would likely give it all away to more or less the same causes! Let him or her give up their lives, I'd rather enjoy mine!

So, what was the reason then, if it wasn't to spend and wasn't to give? Was it to save? Meh...not really. I mean, it would be pretty bad ass to check your ATM card and see nine fucking figures in there, but even I know how ridiculous that would be to have as a goal to base your life around.
In all honesty, I think I wanted to get rich just to get rich. Just to have it beside my name: 'He got really rich'.
I'm embarrassed even admitting that. Or at least I would be, if I didn't know that that's the way a lot of young people feel.

Death was the only person who ever challenged me on that. I told him the charity thing and he called bullshit. I told him the saving thing and he said that once he was finished taking me, I wouldn't even be aware of the money that I'd left behind. I tried to come up with a few more reasons like 'it's the only way of keeping score' and again, he called me out. I eventually asked him why I wanted to make money. He had, after all, seen every human, rich and poor, leave the planet and complete their 'exit interview' with him on the way out.

"You want to make money", he told me, "because you are human. The desire to make money is, in fact, one of the most human traits you have. It is natural. It is instinct. Humans are social mammals. In fact, we are the most social of mammals, in that we have created the most complex and multi-dimensional society within which we operate. Put several male and female gorillas in a confined area and they will, over time, assume a hierarchical structure in their community, particularly if you make them realise that the confined area they share does not contain sufficient resources to sustain all of them in the long run.

And that is exactly what has happened in the case of humanity. We are a collection of social mammals that share finite resources. It is in our nature – under our survival instincts – to try to accumulate as much of this resource for ourselves as we possibly can."

"If that's true", I asked him, "why are there so many people who do not make as much money as they possibly can, who say that they don't want any more?".

"Just because I said it is natural to want money", Death responded, "doesn't mean that money is the *only* natural desire of social mammals. If it was, life would be very boring – we would each spend our entire lives working. We have thousands of other instincts and natural desires to meet and fulfil in our daily lives. The desire for social interaction, personal growth, sex, love, adventure, emotional expression, creative expression, exercise…the list goes on. Modern life – the variety of lives that you see being lived around you – is a reflection of that. The wall street trader, the social entrepreneur and the globetrotting beach bum all have the same primal desires, they just have them in different amounts and in different orders of priority. So next time you see or meet someone and you think 'she is just so different to me, we have such different values', remember that you actually don't. In fact, you have the exact same values, you just weight them differently, and that is what makes this society of ours so interesting."
"You see, when we zoom out, we realise that we are all very similar. It is through the magnifying lens through which we approach day to day life down here that our differences become more conspicuous and significant-seeming. We have so many impulses to just band together and work together for a better overall society, but then we have an equal amount of impulses to compete with one another. Balancing these impulses is at the very core of every human and societal interaction. It has scarcely evolved over the past 2,000 years, nor would it be likely to, were we to have that amount of time left down here."

"So the pursuit of money is not a bad thing. It buys survival, in our society. It buys experiences for us and those that matter to us. It allows us to patron the arts and the causes that matter to us, and it allows us to amplify our own personalities and values unto the world, which is another primal urge of ours."

"But happiness comes from the inside, not from what's going on around you. You notice that the really introspective people – Buddhists, Taoists etc – are not very money-driven. That is because they realise this. Everything you need for happiness and inner peace is inside you already. For that, money is unimportant."

Something that Death has taught me - purely by dragging me as far as the gate so that I could see it – is that the world is really a giant amusement park. It's a playground, with more rides, toys and stimuli than one can fathom - let alone enjoy - in one lifetime. Just like all amusement parks, some of the most appealing rides require coupons. Money is the coupons. However, it is within each of us to get just as much stimulation out of the less attractive rides as we would out of the attractive, expensive ones. That is where the Taoist, Buddhist and other spiritual trainings come in.

Materialism

While Death defends the pursuit of money, he abhors materialism, and he warns against the fine, fine line that separates the two.

Materialism is a simple drug, same as any other. Use it and it can give you a temporary high. Overuse it and it will start to consume you, after which point your values and your life will unravel, the same way it would when consumed by any other drug.
The dangerous thing about money? It provides you with all the apparatus for the consumption of that drug.

I love baked goods, Brownies, biscuit cake; basically anything chocolatey that I can get my hands on. Sometimes I look in the window a café and I just drool at the sight of some of the incredible looking desserts they have in there. And sometimes – maybe a little too often – I tell myself that life is too short and I go in and enjoy one.

And so I should. Someone has put a lot of work into baking that with the sole intention of satisfying a consumer. They have experimented with flavours and textures and all sorts of things, and then they have turned it from food into art by decorating it into a masterpiece. All of the skill that goes into that! That is something to be enjoyed.

But if I were to do that every day, I would quickly become addicted (and fat). I would no longer be stopping at the shop window by choice, but out of necessity. Then, I would stop stopping at the shop window at all – I'd just walk straight in and order the first treat I saw. After that, I would reach a phase where I would no longer even enjoy the desserts I was buying, I would just consume them out of habit, or even require two at a time to give me the same rush that one once did. Stemming on from that, I would likely become overweight, I would be spending crazy amounts of money on biscuit cake, and my mood would suffer if I didn't have any that day. I would suffer in my health (diabetes) and in my relationships (mood swings) and so on and so forth. All because of one simple biscuit cake!?

That is white sugar. And just like white sugar, materialism, too, is a drug with a harmless face.

In fact, I would venture to say that materialism is to the soul what white sugar is to the body. We saw the white sugar spiral above. Here is what the materialism spiral looks like:

Look in the shop window and see a nice item. Treat yourself.
Get complements on the nice item when wearing it and enjoy the social status that it brings – same as the taste of the dessert.

Go back and seek that reward again, just as a once off. Enjoy it again, possibly even more.

Notice someone else's nice item – a different dessert – and feel the need to try that one, just out of curiosity.

Now you're in competition.

Keep coming back and buying so that you can go out and get the same social or personal reward from a new item.

Before you know it, significant money has been spent on clothing/jewellery/car or whatever. The way your mood swings on white sugar, so too does your self-esteem and social confidence swing on materialism. Your finances suffer. Your relationships change with your value weighting (more on image less on substance), and so on.

It is a habit loop. Cue, Habit, Reward, Repeat.

And just like the white sugar habit, this goes full circle. The only way to break the chain is to cut it. Cold turkey. With sugar your moods and energy will fall. With materialism your self- and social worth will fall. But eventually, when enough time has passed, your energy/mood and self/social worth sources will move back off sugar and materialism and back to where they were, or to some other sustainable source.

Brownies are delicious. They are to be eaten.
Nice clothes are beautiful. They are to be worn and enjoyed.
Nice cars are amazing. They are to be driven.
Nice houses are iconic. They are to be lived in.
Nice wine is relaxing. It is to be drank.

These are all marvels of the human hand. It is incredible that our fellow man have created these things to which we react so positively. We should honour their work and their vision by indulging in them – every now again. Overconsumption of any of these treats can put you on a spiral that is extremely difficult and expensive (in more ways than one) to break.

Law of Attraction & Instagram

You know how the Instagram algorithm works, right? You go and click on, comment on or 'like' a bunch of hot girls' photos, your Discovery page will be full of hot girls' photos that you can then explore and find new ones to follow. You interact with food pages, your Discovery will be full of new food pages. Muscle, sport, fashion…same thing.

This, ladies and gentlemen, is the law of attraction made manifest by technology, and the exact same logic and principle applies in the real world. What we click on, like and engage with gets shown to us more and more.

Here's an example of that happening in my real life in Sydney. I love Spanish, always have, and I speak it, although not nearly as often as I'd like.
I met a girl in Google and we got on great. *Click*.
She told me she was Spanish. "You're Spanish!", I shouted in her face, doing as good a job as ever to play it cool. "I love Spanish people!". *Like*.
Somehow she remained talking to me and we got on great. While I think she thought I was a bit crazy, she also appreciated my enthusiasm for her mother tongue (still talking about language here people) – she acknowledged the 'Like'. We're speaking Spanish, talking about Spain etc, and just hitting it off. I tell her what a pleasure it is to speak some Spanish again and that I wish I could speak it more often – *Comment*.
She invites me to a barbecue at her house that weekend with more Spanish people. I go, and there I meet lots of Spanish folk speaking lots of Spanish. As I'm chatting away to a new Spanish friend, I hear someone else behind me talking about how they love tennis.
I turn around. *Click*.
"I love tennis too!" I said. "Where do you play?" *Like*.
"I used to play as a kid but would love to get back into it", I say. *Comment.*
I was playing tennis with him within two weeks.

See how this is working? We build our own world on Instagram by clicking, liking and commenting. We then get frustrated that the world we really live in doesn't quite reflect our interests as much as the Instagram world. I don't think that needs to be the case at all. We build it the same way – Click, Like, Comment – and we get to live the rewards we want ourselves. I clicked, liked and commented on Spanish, and I ended up at a Spanish BBQ. I then clicked, liked and commented on tennis, and ended up playing two weeks later. That's how the algorithm works, right?

Something you should know about life: No one moment is more valuable than another. Is one shit moment worth one good moment? Not necessarily, because they're both moments. It's the lasting moments that we need to look out for. That's where love, charity, relationships etc come in. Having sex with a good looking person, driving a fast car, sleeping in a dope hotel room…they're all cool, but they do fade, and before you know it, you've moved on to another moment, to which the previous moment contributes nothing but elevated expectations.

Aeterna non Caduca is the motto of my old school. It''s Latin for 'The things that last forever, not the things that pass away'. I heard or read that roughly 4 times every day for 6 years as a teenager. I left that school 8 years ago. I have scarcely heard it since. Somehow, it has only really made sense as I write this here in Stephens Green in Dublin on a warm but cloudy Tuesday afternoon. I'm on a bench beside an old couple to the right of the pond.
I think this will be one of the moments that lasts.

Something you should know about Death: I have told this to many people and, when I look at their faces, I know it's not sinking in. Maybe it's like describing the colour red to someone without mentioning any other colours. When you die, you don't know you die. You don't exist anymore, so you can't know. You don't even know you ever lived. You don't know anything. You don't exist. There is no 'You'.
The best way I can describe this (admittedly abstract) concept is by drawing on my own experience. I woke up after dying, being brought back to life, and spending a week in a coma recovering. People ask me what it's like being dead. I have no idea. People ask me what it's like being in a coma. Your guess is as good as mine. People ask me if you 'see anything' when you're dead. No, you don't. You're dead. You don't exist anymore.
What I'm saying is this: Had I not woken up and recovered fully, I would never have known that I'd died. I'd never have known that I'd lived. I'd never have known that I never achieved some goals and did achieve others. I'd never have known I was poor, or rich, or somewhere in the middle. I'd never have known anything. I would simply have been a character in other people's memories.

Now I know what you're thinking. *'This has gotten very deep and very weird very quickly…is there something I should be taking away from this before it makes me dizzy?'*

Yes, there is. When you die, you don't know you die, nor do you know you lived. You don't get to do the full review that people think you do, that people expect to do and that many people base their whole lives on – "I'm going to live life this way because when I die I'll look back and be happy I did it".

Sorry mate, doesn't work that way. When you die you'll be dead. You won't exist anymore, so that review will never happen.

If you die suddenly, you'll have no idea you were about to die, and, like me, you'll go from napping on a tour bus and wrapping up smelly feet to not existing, all in the space of 20 minutes. No review.

If you do have some time before you die, during which you know you're going to die, then you do in fact get a review (provided your brain is functioning well). In this review, you will again go back to the durable elements of your life, not the transient ones. You'll reflect on the commitments you made and the effect you had on other lives, and that is also what you will be remembered for.

I'm totally unequipped to advise on these circumstances seeing as I had the 'surprise' package myself, but Death has advised me to focus on the durables to protect me in this review, and to ensure I enjoy myself and scratch every itch I have while I can, just in case I don't get a review. I guess life is the review. This is continuous assessment, not exam time, only you are both the student and the master of your own life and performance in it.

Scalable Behaviour

All of the world's main issues: Overpopulation, Climate Change, Plastic Oceans, Holy wars….I can't solve any of them. Why not? I'm an educated young guy living in a first world country – there should be no limit to what I can do in this life.

The reason I can't solve these issues is because of Death. Put simply, I won't be around long enough to have the impact that I need to have to solve these things. I can't solve them. So what should I do? Succumb to my inability to singlehandedly solve these issues and just add to them? Continue eating a diet that exhausts resources, continue to use plastic when it's not needed, etc? Sure I could. In fact, that would be the easiest and most comfortable thing to do.

Or, I could behave in a scalable way. That is, I could behave in a way that, if everyone behaved like me, the world would be better off. This applies to every area of life. Where is the low hanging fruit?

- Eat a diet that is better for the planet. You don't have to eliminate meat entirely if you love it. Just reduce your intake. Eat it at lunch and not dinner, or only eat it on weekends, or do no meat Mondays. Who cares, just do something and stick to it. 1lb of beef served requires 12,000 litres of drinking water to produce.
  Twelve. Thousand. Litres. Try to reduce your intake incrementally over time and you won't even notice the difference. Except you'll look better- you'll notice that.
- Use less plastic. Get a reusable coffee cup and water bottle. If everyone did that, it would make an ENORMOUS positive impact on the planet, and wouldn't be at all inconvenient to the people doing it. The amount of plastic we use is totally insane. There is an island in the North Pacific Ocean that is made entirely of plastic and is four times the size of France. I shit you not. All consumer plastic.
- Be nice to strangers, remembering that a stranger to you is a family member to someone else. Treat them as you would like your family members to be treated out in the world by the strangers that they encounter.

The list goes on here, and you know what's required just as well as I do. I'm just trying to remind you to put your best foot forward. You have to decide what that looks like. But if we all made a move to scalable behaviour, the needle would be seriously moved on a lot of things.

Little secret of mine: I want Ireland to be the leader on all of this stuff. We're currently one of the worst on both childhood obesity and plastic and energy use. We're appalling, actually. But with just 5 million people on this tiny island – half of whom are feckin' related if we're being honest – I just feel so strongly that we are in the perfect position to set the standard for Europe on some of the world's leading issues, and I would love for nothing more than to see that happen.

"If it has two legs..."

One can easily picture a little boy, sitting alone on a swing with no friends around him, crying. It's an image that, though sad, seems normal to us. Some kids struggle to make friends and can go years without any. Some kids have terrible home situations that none of the other kids are aware of or could even understand. Some kids just really find it hard to manage in life, for whatever reason. They're that boy on the swing, and we can easily picture that.

That state of mind, though – that loneliness, those struggles, that stuff at home that nobody knows of or could even understand – that is so much more prevalent among adults than it is among kids. Some kids have some stuff going on. Almost every adult does.

I guess the point of this, as a finishing note, is to remind you of that. If you take a minute to think of the last person you saw today, the person you see most consistently every day, and the person you are going to see next; Think about those people and realise that they could well be going through exactly what that boy on the swing is going through. Just remember that when you're dealing with them, and when you're talking to them. Remember it when you're talking to strangers. Remember that, if it has two legs and is a member of society, that *by definition,* it has a complex relationship with itself, it has a complex relationship with its tribe or its family, and it has a complex relationship with the world. By definition. Remember that, when dealing with people. We're very complicated and each and every single one of us in more fragile than we ever let on. Just remember that, and try to be a person that brings just a little smile to every one you come into contact with. That, to me, is a life well-lived

Lifecycles

My parents separated after 27 years together. Society would probably put that down as a failed relationship.

Really? 27 years is a failure?? I disagree. If I started a business and it did really well but then closed down after 27 years, would I be a failed entrepreneur?
Of course not. That is because everything in life, not just life itself, runs in lifecycles. And that lifecycle has a trajectory. Most life-cycles look like distribution graphs, or bell charts, though the long tail can be on either side or not exist at all.

We tend to be sad when things decline or end or change away from what they used to be, particularly when it comes to elements of our life to which we are emotionally attached, like relationships or careers or trips etc. This is totally natural – us getting upset I mean. But it is also totally natural that these things come to an end. Everything dies. If something of nature exists – a relationship, a food, a plant, a business (group of people with a mission) – then it will just as surely die. McDonalds will die, possibly in the next 50 years as we move away from junk food and meat. Coca Cola will definitely die. Nike will die as more disruptors like Under Armour come and take market share from them. Google, Apple, Facebook, they'll all die in time. They will never have failed. They will all have been successful. But they will die.

Why am I going on about this? I'm doing it because it's maybe the most important lesson I've ever learned: the sooner we can get to grips and get comfortable with the certainty of death – and doing so is certainly an unpleasant process, the sooner we get to appreciate what we have in life – we start celebrating the lifecycle what it is there, because it one day won't be.

Life is just a series of lifecycles – micro and macro. Everything comes in waves, and every wave breaks.

Macro lifecycles: Education lifecycle(0-22), Grad lifecycle, travel lifecycle, 'get serious lifecycle', various career lifecycle, young family lifecycle, teenage family lifecycle, winding back lifecycle, adult family lifecycle, retirement lifecycle, grandchildren lifecycle etc.

Micro lifecycle: Yoga lifecycle, Fitness lifecycle, Learning a language lifecycle, 'I hate my job' lifecycles, 'I love my job lifecycles, friendship lifecycles, relationship lifecycles, single lifecycles, live abroad lifecycles, etc.

Many lifeccyles are made up of sub lifecycles, particularly in the relationship sphere. For example, I have a friend who I have known since I was 12, so you could say our relationship lifecycle has gone on 14 years now (wow!). We weren't friends in school, just friendly. Then we left school, and our 'school relationship lifecycle' ended. We embarked on a college relationship lifecycle, where we hung out to drink every now and then. Then I went to Australia, where we developed a new relationship lifecycle, that existed over skype and watsapp. Now we live together, and that is its own relationship lifecycle. Soon he's going travel, so our current lifecycle will die and we another one will grow.

This happens with every relationship we have. It's good to be aware of as it really enables us to manage and perceive change with less confusion and more control and understanding.

Every single thing we do bar basic bodily functions is just part of a wave/lifecycle. As a practice it will come, it will reach a peak of intensity, and it will go. Welcome it when it comes. Enjoy it while it's there and release it without resistance when it goes.

What will the Robots Think?

If you are interested in technology and read about it, you'll be aware of the Singularity Hypothesis, which I'll summarise as the hypothesis that Artificial Intelligence will grow out of the limitations which we thus far know it to have (self-awareness, emotion etc) and surpass the human race as the dominant 'species' on Earth. I am a subscriber to this hypothesis, and I often wonder if our extinction is the only thing that will enable Planet Earth and all of its other millions of species and life types (of which we are only .0000001%, remember) can survive.

What I also wonder in this context is what the robots, if they do take the reins, will think when they look at the evolution and life cycle of humans on Earth. Will they look at how we structured our societies and see that it could have been formed more effectively, in ways we either dismissed or never even thought of? Will they look at how we interreacted with one another and shake their heads, knowing that there was a higher state of being for us had we only treated each other better? Could we have achieved infinitely more had we worked with each other as a global team, sharing our resources, rather than against each other as separate national teams competing for those resources? Will they shake their heads at what a tragedy it was that we couldn't heed the warnings and control our consumption? Will they pity us for our weakness in the face of addictions, like consumerism and sugar and alcohol? Will they laugh at the absence of logic in our obsession with impressing people we don't like or care for, who are secretly trying to impress us in return? Will they sneer at our vehemence on choosing jobs and careers that don't enthuse us; the cause of unnecessary friction and inner turmoil. What will they say about the destruction of our planet? What will they say about our inability to control our weight and the obesity epidemic? What will they think of us when they find out that we knew all along that all of this was unnecessary and that the ingredients for a blissful, healthy and perfectly fulfilling life were not just readily available, but provided for free by nature all around us and inside us?

Humanity is just realising that there's no point to life

I watched Kung Fu panda this morning. I love those animated movies. The way they weave important life lessons into an entertaining story arc is something I don't think I'll ever get bored of.

Anyway, briefly put, the whole crux of the film is that there are two sides trying to get a hold of this scroll that will give them the secret to greatness and happiness and all else that is good in this world. While the movie is meant for kids, I was actually thinking that such a scroll would be much more coveted by adults than by kids, seeing as kids seem to already possess the secret to happiness.

As the plot unfolds, one guy gets the scroll and, expecting to find a summary of the secret to life, he opens it.
It's blank.
No words, nothing. All that he sees a reflection of himself.
In the scene beforehand, the panda asks his father for the thousandth time what the secret ingredient to his delicious 'Special Secret Ingredient Noodle Soup' is. The father tells him "there is no secret ingredient. What makes the soup special is one's belief that it is special".

This all resonated with me on a much deeper level than I'd imagine the brilliant makers of Kung Fu Panda even planned on it resonating with people, and I really think it is so true. It seems that there have been philosophers from the East for hundreds or thousands of years who have realised that there is no point to life; That there is no 'secret to greatness' or 'secret ingredient', and that all that we need in order for something to have special significance, is for us to *believe* that it has special significance.

I feel that while the East have known this for thousands of years, the West have spent that time intensifying their own search for meaning. With the advent of meditation, yoga and Buddhism sweeping through our society now, it appears that people are starting to embrace the fundamentals of Eastern philosophy, or at least include it as a factor in our search for that which doesn't exist. Who knows where this combination will take us, but it does appear that we're starting to get the message.

That 'getting the message' phase is difficult. It's difficult because, when we had a made-up purpose to live for - make money/travel etc – we at least had a path to follow. Then, we reached the tipping point in recordings of people saying that these paths hadn't fulfilled them, and we started looking East for guidance. They told us there is no path (bar the eightfold path), and that the only search worth conducting was inside ourselves. We asked them what the hell that even meant and they asked us to be quiet, they were meditating.

And now we're scrambling. We don't know if we should be meditating or not; We're trying to figure out how to meditate - 'Do I keep my eyes open? Can I meditate while I'm drinking with the lads?' We're quitting jobs, getting divorced, going travelling and trying drugs at a much higher rate than we ever have. All because we're totally lost. Just like Nacho said: take away the title of the assignment and nobody knows what to do.

But I don't think we need to worry. I think this lost phase is a very healthy one, both for humanity as a whole and for the individuals going through it themselves. I met thousands of people in 2017 – thousands! – and not one of them was as lost in this life as I was (apart from this one guy – he's definitely fucked). And I'm glad I went through that. Delighted, actually. It cost money, it was exhausting, and it was extremely worrying and stressful at times, but God I'm happy I went through it. As well as many other things, it enabled me to appreciate what I had, see the whole board for the first time, and come to peace with the fact that I had to choose my own purpose in life – that running with one that was passed to me by someone else was never going to satisfy me.

So, to everyone reading this who is lost and freaking out about it:

1) You're definitely in a better place than I was. As well as having PTSD and wondering if I'd poured all my potential down the drain, I had no idea what I wanted out of life, as I was in the middle of a massive transition of ideals.

2) You being lost might put you at an advantage. The key to being lost is having an open mind. Welcome every idea, every person and every offer/opportunity. A semi-requirement of being focussed is having a somewhat closed mind. If you are below 30 and have never opened up your mind completely – the way you do when you're lost or travelling or whatever – then you're probably at a disadvantage, because you've never looked outside your path at the million other paths on offer in life. Doing this isn't just beneficial if you're looking to change paths, it's beneficial because you get a better understanding and perspective of the path you're on in a broader context, and you get a better understanding of the person you are and are becoming on that path. If you're lost and you've got that open mind, indulge it as much as you can (safely), and you'll eventually find a path after a much more thorough search (remember the axe story in part 2?)

3) Better to get lost and confused now in your twenties than later in your fifties when you have dependents who rely on you to be stable. If you've never been confused, that could be an issue.

Getting lost in your twenties is a very healthy and positive thing. I wrote an article about it once called 'Positive Confusion'. The confusion feels extremely negative, but it's a blessing, trust me. Indulge it, enjoy it, and trust it to send you on the right path *for you*.

Fuel the Spirit

As I came toward the end of this book, I had a realisation. I'd added so much time on to my work day, just thinking, planning and writing this thing. People would ask why and whether it was for the money. No, books don't make money, everyone knows that. Was it for the attention? No. If I'm honest with myself, this book has a low probability of even achieving that much attention – most books don't – so to invest that much in a long shot would be irrational.

So what was it for then? I thought and thought about this, and I realised that I just did it because it makes me feel alive. It fuels my brain a little bit, definitely doesn't fuel my body, but it absolutely fuels my soul, my spirit. I thought about that then and thought about what else fuels the spirit. I landed on music – what makes you feel more alive – what makes that fire inside you burn brighter – than a great song or a moving song delivered at the right time. I thought about movies. I thought about travelling the world and the feeling I get when I arrive in new places for the first time. I thought about work, and how that can really ignite my fire since I started doing jobs I actually liked and was designed for. I thought about relationships, meeting new people, doing interesting activities, even just once. These are all things that throw fuel on the little fire that burns inside every one of us, and I have realised that these – that that – is the number one most important thing in life. There's a little candle light inside you. Sometimes if you go through a rough period or you do a job you hate, the flame gets smaller and smaller and threatens to go out. When it does go out, that's when you're in a rut and you need to take some massive action to change your environment or circumstances. But sometimes that flame roars, and turns into this inferno that you can barely control – and they are the moments we live for.

Does money help? Sure, money can pay for some things that can really fuel the soul, like skydiving or cool concerts. But more the most part – and I mean 95% of – the things that fuel our soul, are absolutely free. Laughs, music, doing things we're scared of, challenges, adventures, talking to strangers...you don't need to be rich for any of these things. Fuel your soul, and you'll have an incredible life.

Death taught me that.

Ending

If there's one thing that I hope you've gotten from this book, it's this:

I hope this book has helped you to realise that there really is nothing to be afraid of in life.

I generally operate on the assumption that we'll all go through a tough time every couple of years. That's part of life. If it didn't happen, we wouldn't grow, we wouldn't quite appreciate the many good times we have, and we wouldn't be forced to reflect on who we are and where we're going; given the opportunity to make changes when necessary.
There's nothing in life that is worth being afraid of. Every pain subsides and you generally come out stronger, eventually seeing why you needed to go through that pain to get to where you were destined to go and be who you were destined to be. Every social norm that we are afraid of not sticking to, was the output of someone else's thinking and not our own, so sticking to it may not be in our interests at all. Remember, not everyone who wanders is lost. Every 'life' that you are afraid of leaving – relationships, jobs, countries – has another life waiting for you beyond the horizon, a life that is probably more suited to the new, updated version of you. Every bright future lies beyond the horizon – further than the eye can see. All we can do is part from the comfort of the shore and start sailing towards it. It'll be rough and stormy at times and you'll often feel like turning back. Don't. Trust that the storms are developing you into the person you'll need to be when you get there. If the wind throws you off the course that you'd planned for yourself, don't worry. Trust that that wind has a better understanding of where you need to go than you do. You will get there, one way or another. All you need to focus on is persevering through the storms, trusting the wind and enjoying the ride.

The people around you whose opinions feed into your choices – they're just people who happen to be alive during the same speck of time as you are. They have nothing to do with your journey.

When it comes to relationships and work, never sign up for anything you're not excited about.

And last of all, don't die wondering.

35747893R00065

Printed in Poland
by Amazon Fulfillment
Poland Sp. z o.o., Wrocław